Bion and Intuition in the Clinical Setting

Bion and Intuition in the Clinical Setting focuses on Bion's investigation of the intuitive approach to clinical data and lays out how Bion's method encouraged constant effort by the analysts to relinquish its reliance on sensory and conceptual-verbal faculties to make room for intuition.

Based on the work of the biannual Bion conference, this book includes contributions from the most eminent voices on Bion's work. Spanning topics such as the primordial mind, intuitive comprehension and desire, the contributors in this volume illustrate how they incorporate the concept of intuition in their own clinical developments. Each chapter examines different elements of how Bion's research approaches the difficulties faced by analysts in the approach and discrimination of primitive emotional levels in the patient-analyst communication.

This book will be of key interest to analysts and analytic therapists of all schools and is an essential resource for those that follow the work of Bion.

Antònia Grimalt, M.D., is a training and supervising analyst for the Spanish Society (SEP-IPA) and the Spanish Federation of Associations of Psychotherapists (FEAP), as well as a child and adolescent training analyst for the former Hans Groen Prakken Institute (EPI). She is former Chair of the Forum for Child Psychoanalysis (FEP) and is a member of the Ed. Monografies de Psicoanàlisi i Psicoteràpia. She has taught on the works of Klein and Bion at multiple universities, and has edited works on Bion, Pere Folch, Matte Blanco and Ricardo Lombardi in both Spanish and Catalan. In 2020, she chaired the International Bion Meeting in Barcelona.

'Of reading the papers in this book we could paraphrase Bion: "the object of such extra-sessional work is to provide practice, analogous to the musician's scales and exercises, to sharpen and develop intuition". A community of 400 analysts gathered in a warm Barcelona, from Europe and worldwide. With them they brought considerable clinical experience, the testing and utilisation of which was sharpened by our "extra-sessional work" together at the conference, and now in the perhaps calmer waters of personal reading.'

Nicola Abel-Hirsch, *author of Bion: 365 Quotes (2019)*
and a training analyst of the British Psychoanalytical Society, UK

'In the evolving tradition of memorializing the findings of the bi-annual International Bion Congress, we have a solid contribution from the Bion in Barcelona Congress of 2020. Just like its predecessor, Alisobhani and Corstorphine's *Explorations in Bion's "O"*, which commemorated the work of the Bion in Los Angeles Congress of 2014, Antònia Grimalt's editing of *Bion and Intuition in the Clinical Setting*, delivers exactly what is promised in its title: the work of analysts who have deployed Bion's various epistemological ideas in the analytic situation. Many contributions center on extrapolating the meaning of Bion's often quoted idea: the abandonment of memory and desire in the consulting room. Clearing one's mind of obstructive impediments to direct contact paves the way for the operation of intuition in all the many faceted ways demonstrated by a talented group of analysts.'

Joseph Aguayo, *member of the New Center for Psychoanalysis,*
Los Angeles; Guest Member of the British Psychoanalytical
Society and member of the Psychoanalytic Center of
California, Los Angeles, USA

The Routledge Wilfred Bion Studies Book Series

Series Editor Howard B. Levine, MD

Editorial Advisory Board

Nicola Abel-Hirsch, Joseph Aguayo, Avner Bergstein, Lawrence J. Brown, Judith Eekhoff, Claudio Laks Eizerik, Robert D. Hinshelwood, Chris Mawson, James Ogilvie, Elias M. da Rocha Barros, Jani Santamaria, Rudi Vermote

The contributions of Wilfred Bion are among the most cited in the analytic literature. Their appeal lies not only in their content and explanatory value, but in their generative potential. Although Bion's training and many of his clinical instincts were deeply rooted in the classical tradition of Melanie Klein, his ideas have a potentially universal appeal. Rather than emphasizing a particular psychic content (e.g., Oedipal conflicts in need of resolution; splits that needed to be healed; preconceived transferences that must be allowed to form and flourish, etc.), he tried to help open and prepare the mind of the analyst (without memory, desire or theoretical preconception) for the encounter with the patient.

Bion's formulations of group mentality and the psychotic and non-psychotic portions of the mind, his theory of thinking and emphasis on facing and articulating the truth of one's existence so that one might truly learn first hand from one's own experience, his description of psychic development (alpha function and container/contained) and his exploration of O are "non-denominational" concepts that defy relegation to a particular school or orientation of psychoanalysis. Consequently, his ideas have taken root in many places . . . and those ideas continue to inform many different branches of psychoanalytic inquiry and interest.[1]

It is with this heritage and its promise for the future developments of psychoanalysis in mind that we present *The Routledge Wilfred Bion Studies Book Series*. This series gathers together under newly emerging and continually evolving contributions to psychoanalytic thinking that rest upon Bion's foundational texts and explore and extend the implications of his thought. For a full list of titles in the series, please visit the Routledge website at: www.routledge.com/The-Routledge-Wilfred-Bion-Studies-Book-Series/book-series/RWBSBS.

Howard B. Levine, MD Series Editor

Note

1 Levine, H.B., and Civitarese, G. (2016). Editors' Preface. In H.B. Levine and G. Civitarese (Eds.), *The W.R. Bion Tradition*. London: Karnac, p. xxi.

Bion and Intuition in the Clinical Setting

Edited by Antònia Grimalt

Routledge
Taylor & Francis Group

LONDON AND NEW YORK

Cover image: Joan Miró, Bleu III, 1961 © Successió Miró, 2021

First published 2022
by Routledge
4 Park Square, Milton Park, Abingdon, Oxon OX14 4RN

and by Routledge
605 Third Avenue, New York, NY 10158

Routledge is an imprint of the Taylor & Francis Group, an informa business

British Library Cataloguing-in-Publication Data
A catalogue record for this book is available from the British Library

Library of Congress Cataloging-in-Publication Data
A catalog record for this book has been requested

ISBN: 978-1-032-27576-5 (hbk)
ISBN: 978-1-032-26950-4 (pbk)
ISBN: 978-1-003-29338-5 (ebk)

DOI: 10.4324/9781003293385

Typeset in Times New Roman
by Apex CoVantage, LLC

To my sons and grandsons

Contents

Acknowledgments

Intuition

The intuitive mind is a sacred Gift.
And the rational mind is a faithful Servant.
We have created a Society that honors the servant.
and has forgotten the Gift.

(Albert Einstein)

This book about intuition in clinical practice springs of contributions of the XI International Bion Conference in 2020, illustrated with clinical material. It examines the many ways in which the authors conceive the concept of intuition in their clinical developments.

All the components of the local Organizing and Scientific Committee spent many hours over two and a half years, meeting and dreaming the Bion 2020 XI Conference into being: a patience and constancy for which plenty of gratitude is owed to Esperança Castell, Josep Oriol Esteve, Elena Fieschi, Lluis Isern, Jose Antonio Loren, Carmen Miranda, Montserrat Pol, Mabel Silva, Carlos Tabbia, and Maria Alicia Vinent. In particular, I am grateful for the valuable suggestions by Giorgio Corrente, with his long experience in the organization of Bion congresses. Special mention goes to my small Bion study seminar (E. Castell, L.L. Isern, M. Pol, M. Silva, and A. Vinent) for its unflagging work discussing the congress papers.

All my gratitude goes also to Howard B. Levine, the Routledge's Bion Series Editor, for his great help in providing guidelines for selecting and editing the papers to be published. To Chris Mawson (recently deceased) and Nicola Abel-Hirsch for their help finding quotations from Bion in New York and Sao Paulo. Finally, I would like to stress the enthusiasm that the theme of the congress aroused, reflected in the quantity, quality, and depth of individual papers we received, which was twice as many as we had been able to include in the present volume, given the time and space available. We are grateful to all the contributors.

About the editors and contributors

Guido Berdini is a psychoanalyst and member of the *Società Psicoanalitica Italiana* (*SPI* – Italian Psychoanalytical Society) and the International Psychoanalytical Association (IPA). He lives in Rome, where he works as a psychologist in the Italian National Health Service. He specializes in clinical psychology and psychotherapy with groups and individuals.

Ilan Bernat, Ph.D. is a training and supervising analyst and faculty member at the Israel Psychoanalytic Society. He teaches seminars on the writings of Bion at the Israel Winnicott Centre and in the postgraduate track in psychotherapy at Tel Aviv University, School of Medicine, 'The Independent Current in Psychoanalysis'. He has a private practice in psychoanalysis and psychotherapy for adults and adolescents in Israel.

Celia Fix Korbivcher is Full Member, Supervisor, and Child Analyst at the Brazilian Psychoanalytic Society of São Paulo.

Antònia Grimalt, M.D., is a training and supervising analyst for the Spanish Society (SEP-IPA) and the Spanish Federation of Associations of Psychotherapists (FEAP), as well as a child and adolescent training analyst for the former Hans Groen Prakken Institute (EPI). She is former Chair of the Forum for Child Psychoanalysis (FEP) and is a member of the Ed. Monografies de Psicoanàlisi i Psicoteràpia. She has taught on the works of Klein and Bion at multiple universities, and has edited works on Bion, Pere Folch, Matte Blanco and Ricardo Lombardi in both English and Catalan. In 2020, she chaired the International Bion Meeting in Barcelona.

Alicia Beatriz Dorado de Lisondo is a training analyst and teacher (Gep Campinas and SBPSP), child and adolescent psychoanalyst and member of the IPA. She is a member of the GPPA (Prisma Group of Psychoanalysis and Autism) and a co-coordinator in the Adoption Workshop/SBPSP. She is an analyst with training functions at GEP and the SBPSP, member of ALOBB.

Naly Durand, is a full member of the Psychoanalytic Society of Mendoza, Argentina, a psychoanalyst with a specialty in didactic function and child and adolescent psychiatry, and she is affiliated with the IPA.

Joanne Emmens is a psychoanalytic psychotherapist and lecturer from New Zealand, currently working at Ashburn Clinic.

Teresa Rocha Leite Haudenschild is a training analyst and a child and adolescent analyst with the Brazilian Psychoanalytical Society of São Paulo, and a full member of the International Psychoanalytical Association. She has been working in the field of early symbolization, and the constitution of identity and psychosexuality. She has published papers on these topics in Brazilian, Latin-American, and European journals and collections. She published the book: *The First Gaze – Initial psychic development, deficit and autism* in 2015 and *Psychosexualities – Femininity, masculinity and gender* in 2016, by Escuta Ed.

Howard B. Levine is a member of APSA, PINE, and the Contemporary Freudian Society, is on the faculty of the NYU postdoctoral contemporary Freudian track, the editorial board of the *IJP* and *Psychoanalytic Inquiry*, editor-in-chief of the *Routledge Wilfred Bion Studies Book Series*, and in private practice in Brookline, Massachusetts. He has authored many articles, book chapters, and reviews on psychoanalytic process and technique and the treatment of primitive personality disorders. His co-edited books include *Unrepresented States and the Construction of Meaning* (Karnac 2013); *On Freud's Screen Memories* (Karnac 2014); *The Wilfred Bion Tradition* (Karnac 2016); *Bion in Brazil.* (Karnac 2017), and *Andre Green Revisited: Representation and the Work of the Negative* (Karnac 2018). He is the author of *Transformations de l'Irreprésentable* (Ithaque 2019).

Maria Adelaide Lupinacci, M.D., is a full member and training analyst of the Italian Psychoanalytic Society (SPI), a child and adolescent analyst, a full member of the IPA, and former chair of the Child and Adolescent Committee of the training Institute of the SPI. Interested in exploring early states of mind in development and pathology, psychoanalytic clinic, and technical problems, for many years she has led a study group on the work of Bion in Rome. She published a book titled *Analyst pain and psychoanalytic method* (Astrolabio 2015), has contributed chapters in books such as *Una ferita all'origine* (Borla 2012), *Talking with couples* (Karnac Books 2015), *Women and creativity* (Karnac 2014), and published articles in journals on the Oedipus complex, transference and countertransference, guilt, space and time in mental life, and different topics related to Bion. She is in private practice in Rome.

Guelfo Margherita, M.D., is a psychiatrist, SPI-IPA psychoanalyst, and functional trainer at IIPG. In the 1970s, as Chief Psychiatrist, he opened up his asylum department to the territory, through psychoanalytically oriented experiences of territorial psychiatry and group psychotherapy of psychosis. He studied in California and India for many years. Besides working at his clinical practice, he taught at the "Federico II" university in Naples, both in psychology classes and in the Psychiatry Specialization School. He conducts experiential groups, supervisions, consultancies, and interventions in universities and healthcare (psychiatric departments) institutions. He was the referent in group psychoanalysis for the EFPP and a member of scientific committees for organizing various international meetings. His main interest is in the question: "how do institutional and group minds feel, think and operate?"

Ruby Mariela Mejia Maza, M.D., is a psychoanalytic psychotherapist born in Perú. She is also a Training and Supervising Analyst of the Italian Institute of Group Psychoanalysis (IIPG) and an associate member of the Italian Society of Psychoanalytical Psychotherapy (SIPP). She is also a docent at both training institutes. She is a member of the European Federation for Psychoanalytic Psychotherapy (EFPP) and a lecturer in Spanish at the University of Catania. She has a private practice in psychotherapy in Sicily, Italy.

Fulvio Mazzacane is a psychiatrist and a training and supervising analyst at SPI (Italian Psychoanalytic Society) and IPA, as well as President of Pavia Psychoanalytic Center (CPdP).

Mariângela Mendes de Almeida, MA (Tavistock Clinic and UEL), Ph.D. (UNIFESP), is a psychologist and psychotherapist, candidate at SBPSP, member of GPPA, and coordinator of the parent-infant services in the pediatrics department at UNIFESP.

Silvia Neborak is a psychoanalyst specializing in training functions and member of APdeBA. She also teaches at APdeBA, the Psychoanalytic Society of Mendoza, in Madrid, and at the Chilean Psychoanalytic Society. She is also a member of ALOBB.

Alexandre Patouillard is a candidate in analitycs training, member of T.I.R.A.M.I.S.U.-Study Group of Napoli and CRPG of Napoli. He trained in France in "L'Ange Bleu" association on the subject of pedophile and sexual abuse of children.

Antonio Pérez-Sánchez is a psychiatrist and psychoanalyst, training analyst and supervisor at the Spanish Psychoanalytical Society (SEP), and he teaches at SEP Institute. He is a former president of SEP (2008 to 2011). He has published *Elementos de Psicoterapia Breve Psicoanalítica* (1992), *Prácticas Psicoterapéuticas. Psicoanálisis Aplicado a la Asistencia Pública* (1996), *Análisis Terminable* (1997), *Interview and Indicators in Psychoanalysis and Psychotherapy* (Spanish, 2006; English, 2012; Italian, 2014; Spanish, 2nd edition, 2019); *Psicoterapia breve psicoanalítica* (2014), and *Psychotic Organization of the Personality*, English, 2018; Spanish, 2018). Currently he is Chair of the Sponsoring Committee of the International Psychoanalytical Association for the study group Nucleo Portuguese Psicoanalitico (Lisbon). He is a member of the European team of the *Inter-Regional Encyclopedic Dictionary of Psychoanalysis* (International Psychoanalytical Association).

Federico Pone is a psychologist, member of T.I.R.A.M.I.S.U.-Study Group of Napoli, member of CRPG of Napoli and associate founder of APS Psychologist in contact with the non-profit organization.

Salvatore Rotondi is a psychologist, member of   T.I.R.A.M.I.S.U.-Study Group of Napoli, member of CRPG of Napoli and associate founder of APS Psychologist in contact with the non-profit organization.

Jani Santamaria Linares is a training analyst and supervisor of child and adolescent analysis at the Mexican Psychoanalytic Association (APM). She has been a Latin American representative board IPA member 2019–2021, director of community and culture for FEPAL (2016–2018), chair of the International Bion Conference 2022, chair of Latin American Meeting on Winnicott in Mexico 2017, member of the International Advisory Committee: Routledge Bion Studies Book Series, a Latin American book reviewer for *JAPA*, and a member of the International Committee of Spanish Language Psychoanalysts.

Loredana Vecchi is a former psychiatrist manager in the Territorial Services of the DSM of the ASL of Benevento, psychotherapist associated with IIPG, member of the T.I.R.A.M.I.S.U.-Study Group of Naples. She conducts institutional psychotherapy supervision in the Benevento area.

Introduction

The right interpretation . . . will depend on the analyst's capacity . . . to observe that two verbally identic statements are psychoanalytically different.

(Bion, 1963)

The difficulties that the analyst meets in the approach and discrimination of primitive emotional levels in the patient-analyst communication are the focus of Bion's research: at stake, are alpha function and the theory of transformations as an observational method of the phenomena embedded in the analytic encounter.

Evolution takes place in layers, like the layers of an onion. Between each layer there are caesuras that have to be crossed in order to establish a dialogue between both levels. Bion proposes to look for a method that makes possible the encounter and a reflective dialogue between primitive prenatal protomental aspects and post-natal positions, or in other words between the basic assumption group and the working group, between the primitive mind and the differentiated mind. His insistence in taking into account all the coexisting aspects of the personality (not necessarily pathological, including for example what he calls the embryonic intuition) drives him to bring up the perspective of considering the adult as an adult "minus child", or "minus baby" or "minus fetus or embryo", giving rise to the possibility of observing, intuiting, or even guessing about what is lacking, silent or belongs in the area of the negative and helping the integration and the passage between caesuras. In this passage between caesuras, Bion makes the conjecture that the same prenatal forces that push the fetus to free itself from its sensations-(proto)ideas-(proto)emotions, are active and always present. If so, then inaccessible fine archaic thoughts may erupt, with the risk that instead of being transformed through containment, the emotional turbulence may lead to catastrophe (Grimalt, 2006).

There has been a growing recognition in recent years that Bion's World War I traumatic experiences have been a hidden order in his published psychoanalytic writing. The theme of war and references to the military became apparent as an organizing motif beginning in Bion's first publication in 1940, "The 'War of Nerves", and continued through his last article nearly 40 years later, "Making the

DOI: 10.4324/9781003293385-1

best of a bad job", in which we are witness to his awareness of disrupted thinking while under fire, either in the cacophony of battle or in the analyst's consulting room, "When two personalities meet, [and] an emotional storm is created" (Brown, 2019).

From the perspective of his war experience, Bion's proposal of alpha function, can be considered the culmination of several seemingly disconnected facets of his life, all of which had to do with how the mind may process unthinkably painful feelings. His experiences also taught him about the importance of dreaming in order to distinguish between reality and phantasy. Endless bombardment and the deafening roar of battle resulted in sleep deprivation, so that even though one might manage to sleep "when you awoke you wondered whether you were dreaming" (Bion F. 1997).

Reading his war diaries, one has the impression of hearing about a mind that is struggling to dream a horror that cannot be dreamed in the sense of turning it into a memory that may perhaps be repressed; the boundaries between wakefulness and sleep are blurred and "the most appalling dreams . . . are much nicer than the actual reality". Bion has a first-hand sampling of the unending mental agony that can result when dream-work not only fails to disguise, but also is unable to function at all.

Bion was acutely aware of the apparent divide between knowledge that accrues by knowing a thing through sense experience (transformations in K) and experiencing that aspect of the object which "lacks contours and boundaries" (transformations in O). The notion that the analyst and analysand begin each session without memory and desire, unhitched from the past and expectations for the future, introduces a sort of riddle: the analytic couple is challenged to apprehend what is essentially unknowable and to begin that quest from a point of ignorance, separated from what one believes one knows. This is an anxiety provoking situation for analyst and patient who may find some comfort in believing that one knows what is about to happen or what has already occurred. In *Transformations* Bion (1965) expresses his skepticism about the K link and is critical of any model of interpretation that requires that it "should be associated with a K link; the analyst is concerned to understand the associations and to communicate that understanding to the patient" (p. 129). Bion avers that this clinical approach only yields knowledge *about* the patient, not *of* the patient, and can induce an accumulation of facts that may lead the analyst into mistakenly believing that he *understands* the analysand.

For Bion, transformations in K (TK) are an incomplete step in the process of interpretation. Bion called "hearsay", the information about the history of the patient, since such information offers factual details that may be unrelated to the session under observation. Instead, historical material may offer insight into the model of the patient in the analyst's mind. However, TK "does not produce growth, [and] only permits accretions of knowledge about growth" (1965 p. 156). In contrast, Bion states Transformations in O, TO, "cover the domain of [emotional] reality and becoming . . . and are related to growth in becoming" (p. 156).

But what does it mean to truly understand the analysand in ways that promote mental growth? Bion considers experiencing one's emotional truth as being as necessary to personal growth as food is to one's corporeal self. While this statement may seem obvious, Bion observes that *becoming* one's emotional experience may evoke a certain kind of resistance manifested by the analysand's accepting the interpretation in order to know something (TK), yet not feel it (i.e., become it); what Bion terms a resistance to transform $K \rightarrow O$: "transformations in K are feared when they threaten the emergence of transformations in O. . . . Resistance to an interpretation is resistance against change from K to O" (Bion 1965, p. 158).

Bion contrasts one model of technique, "associated with a K link" (p. 129), which directs the analyst to sift through the patient's associations in order to detect hidden, unconscious themes that are then communicated to the analysand. This is the so-called classical analytic approach to neurosis that yields knowledge (K) about the analysand but does not necessarily result in emotional growth. Instead, Bion views the analyst's interpretation as the beginning of a process: one's interpretation is seen as a preconception that awaits the patient's associations, which then saturate the interpretation with meaning. In classical technique, the analysand's associations to the interpretation are considered to confirm, refute or amend the intervention, but here Bion is asserting that the patient's associations serve to further infuse the analyst's interpretation with meaning. Interpretations, in this second model, are part of an intersubjective spiraling process by which the mutual associations of analyst and analysand broaden and deepen their unconscious elaborations of the emotional experience of the clinical hour. Aware of this difference, we can say that Bion's theoretical interests shifted from an epistemological approach towards one that acknowledged the nature of emotional growth, O, and the importance of intuitive processes.

In order to work in this way, it is important to exercise the suppression of memory, desire, and understanding, favoring the act of faith. The latter does not belong to the K system, but to the O system. It is a faith in the importance and reality of a psychoanalytic experience, which is essential to bring about deep psychic change, although its full content remains ineffable. The analyst must be interested in grasping the *evolution* of this reality in the session when it *emerges from the dark and formless void with the evanescent character of dreams*.

Bion (1962) describes a process that acts on primitive emotions to transform them into the basis of dreamlike thoughts that lead to creative communication with oneself and with others. Each stage of this process depends at all times on the links of love (L), hate (H) and the desire to know (K) and coexists with an antithetical process in parallel that he defines as propaganda, lies and basic assumptions disguised as thought that, in reality, propagate false knowledge (- K). The first depends on the container-contained relationship, the use of reverie and alpha function by the mother or analyst, on the bonds of love, hate and knowledge, and the dialectical, oscillating relationship between the schizo-paranoid and the depressive position. What is called O (raw untransformed experience) as unknown experience has to become a personal O transformed by thought. This is not easy. The pain involved in recognizing and tolerating the reality of our experience makes it possible to revert to hallucinosis.

At the base of the concept of transformation is the idea that "thinking thoughts", that is to say to accept new and strange contents, exposes the individual in the same sensation of danger as the one that one has in front of the risk of the psychotic catastrophe, for the disorganization of the knowledge and previous beliefs that it supposes.

Bion's journey in his discovery of alpha function has traveled a long distance from its initial beginnings as an inquiry into how the psyche can learn to think under fire and manage unbearable emotional experience. It moves from there to his realization that another mind is required and, finally, to how the activity of these collaborative minds is internalized as the apparatus for thinking. What distinguishes the discussion of container/contained in *Attention and Interpretation* from previous accounts is Bion's frank depiction of the stresses on the analytic pair associated with the transformation of O as an intersubjective process. Bion states that patients "experience pain but not suffering. . . . The patient may say he suffers but this is only because he does not know what suffering is and mistakes pain for suffering it" (Bion 1965).

But the patient does not suffer alone; the analyst "can, and indeed must, suffer" (1970, p. 19) the analysand's pain, just as a mother intuitively dials into her baby's inarticulate cries, becomes that pain and gives it a name through her reverie.

Bion asserts we must use our intuition and "speculative imagination" to grab hold of unconscious communications that may, at first glance, seem ridiculous or incomprehensible. However, and this is where Bion moves into new territory, he considers these "wild" and "stray" thoughts as indicating that the analyst's mind (alpha function) is in the process of transforming the analysand's unconscious communication. Thus, theory of O is linked with a sense of an evolving unknown in the session and emphasizes the use of the analyst's intuition as a tool for slowly grasping that unknown.

Given that the emotional landscape to be explored by the analytic dyad is the befogged and shadowy territory of O, then the analyst's intuition becomes his chief tool in probing a mental space that is unknowable. In this connection, Bion revisits his earlier (1967b) assertion that the analyst must eschew "memory and desire" to achieve a receptive state of mind, which he now relates to intuition: "For any who have been used to remembering what patients say and to desiring their welfare, it will be hard to entertain the harm to analytic intuition that is inseparable from any memories and any desires" (Bion 1970, p. 31).

Ilan Bernat emphasizes the method of negation, explicitly developed by Bion, designed to free psychoanalytic observation from its reliance on sensory and conceptual-verbal faculties, as almost exclusive means for grasping mental reality. The negation not only of the sensory perception system but also of all secondary process functions in the conscious mind, which creates a movement that provides the possibility of transcending caesuras, through binocular vision in continuous contact with the evolution. Sustainable psychoanalytic discoveries are the result of a steady effort of *negation*, which enables the analyst's and the patient's continuous contact with the evolution – with the kind of emotional memory and experiential knowledge that is revealed intuitively. Bion's method involves constant efforts by the analyst's consciousness to negate its reliance on these faculties, *to* "make room" for intuition.

In Freud's model, negating the sensory perception of the external object is required for the establishment of internal representations. This implies the negation not only of the sensory perception system, but also of all secondary process functions in the conscious mind

What would the mental state be that is most likely to replace the mental saturation resulting from "attachment" to memories, wishes and previous "understandings"? The word that would approximately convey what Bion means, is "faith". Faith in the existence of "an ultimate reality – the unknown, unknowable, 'formless infinite'", out of which only a small portion can be known during an analytical session. As A. Perez Sanchez points out in his chapter, this faith, characteristic of scientific endeavor, "must be distinguished from the religious meaning with which it is invested in conversational usage". In other words, only when disrobed of all artifice, lacking any sense of "anticipation", not *saturated* by memories, desires or previous "understandings", only then can an analytical session take place and "evolve" in an atmosphere of scientific truth.

During the course of a session, the analytic couple deals with numerous competing "configurations" waiting to be seen. Some of them, insofar as they *are* deeply steeped in pleasure or pain, are liable to impose themselves more quickly than others: the meanings they express are immediate, almost self-evident. Such bring us to the subject of hallucinosis, a mental state colonized by the sensuous dimension, by protosensations and by protoemotions that have yet to undergo an alphabetization: the mental event turns into sensuous impressions producing pleasure or pain; meaning is lost and is no longer available for exploration. It could happen that a memory becomes so possessed by a "desire" belonging to a constellation of thought associated with feelings of "grievance, regret, or remorse" that mental growth is precluded. As Berdini points out in his chapter, maintaining an empty and unsaturated state of mind allows a transformative "space" to exist. One that can generate continuous crisscrossing references to meaning based on invariants. To this, the oscillating processes PS↔D, Container-Contained ($\female$ $\male$) and Negative Capability ↔ Selected Fact all contribute. If the analyst is to come into contact with the patient's hallucinosis, (s)he cannot avoid abandoning his/her own personal hallucinosis sustained by memory and desire:

> it is necessary that the analyst undergoes in his own personality the transformation O→K. By eschewing memories, desires, and the operations of memory he can approach the domain of hallucinosis and of the 'acts of faith' by which alone he can become at one with his patients' hallucinations and so effect transformations O→K.
>
> (Bion, 1970, p. 250)

Ruby Mariela Mejia Maza reflects on the factors that can help to clarify the "opacities yet to be identified" and the movements that promote the development of the analyst's reliance on intuition as one of the "organs of emotions", e-motions understood as actions, whose development can be observed only in the process itself. Through a group analysis experience within the analytic field model developed in Italian psychoanalysis, she centers on the observation of experiences of fusionality and tenderness that can favor the appearance of intuition.

In our practice, we are constantly immersed in a continuous flow of what Bion compared to the mystical Alpheus River. The flow is moving in different directions, with turbulence and catastrophic change. As with any other type of growth, we cannot capture it through understanding, but we can let ourselves experience it from a mental state that can approach the infinite. It means that we *should only allow O finding K*. One cannot try to make it happen, but rather just allow it to happen. This is the interesting theme that J. Santamaria Linares develops in her chapter: What is required from the analyst to make contact with the "psychoanalytic objects" is to be capable of staying in mental intuitive states triggering "psychic movement".

Bion's playful suggestion of the "two-way traffic" metaphor, pointing out that rather than writing a book on "the interpretation dreams", one should instead write a book on "*The Interpretation of 'Facts'*" is the focus of Emmens's chapter: the necessary defense to withdraw from and shield ourselves from "reality" and the epistemological instinct that drives us towards truth seeking, constitute an internal "tug of war" tension that exists in us all.

Reverie is the expression of a common area shared by patient and therapist. It is the result of a joint construction that gives voice to protoemotions in search of a representation. Mazzacane considers intuition as the first pole of reverie. It gradually becomes the main tool of analytic work, the only way to solve the problem of the mind's inadequacy in grasping the dynamics of mental states. It permits the capture of thoughts which exist before the thinker, the ultimate reality whose existence is independent of the senses and cannot be empirically verified. The second pole of reverie as a narrative texture like the story we develop in the session, giving form to a note out of tune, to a communicative anomaly, creating a narrative function for that which is devoid of meaning. The analyst's intuition arises from verbal and non-verbal elements, but it is by means of words that the analyst gives form to intuition and starts the processes of thinking.

The "primordial mind", is basically a common theme of the chapters about child analysis:

Mothers, use the "motherese" prosody to communicate with their babies as a model close to Bion's notion of transformations in O. What is relevant is not the content and meaning of the words. The emotion of the mother is translated by the rhythm and intonation of her voice, her facial expression, her muscle tone when carrying the baby, etc. This kind of language will call up the baby to the contact with the mother. This interaction is linked by a "language of emotion". Music is a sensory pathway of communication between patient and analyst, although sometimes also operates as a protective barrier against the vulnerability caused by the conscience of the analyst as a separate person.

When facing patients with predominant autistic states, the analyst himself is exposed to experiences of non-existence. This experience is difficult to bear and requires him to operate with his negative capability (Bion, 1970). For the analyst to penetrate the patient's autistic barrier, he (the analyst) needs to use the same sensory language of the patient as a mean of creating a sensorial link between both. This experience would favor the patient to feel less threatened in the presence of the analyst – a separate person – and eventually encourage the patient to abandon his autistic maneuvers in order to initiate a protocommunication between them. Celia Fix concludes in her chapter the analyst facing transformations in O shares with the patient an intense emotional experience in which a true mood of great intimacy prevails beyond words, an experience that can only be lived and cannot be known. This experience, as she suggests, has the same characteristics of the language of the motherese prosody with her baby.

Alicia Beatriz Dorado de Lisondo, Naly Durand, and Mariângela Mendes de Almeida, in their chapter on the primordial mind and possible links with intuition, underline the capacity and training to be able to sustain the inner earthquake and upside-down turmoil in our own and our patients' primitive experiences, as an expressive and fruitful field for intuition and perhaps a precondition for it to emerge. *From clinical material* touching different levels of mental states, come the questions: Could it be that these prenatal sensations do not always reach the possibility of symbolic expression in verbal, preverbal, artistic language, and may then be compulsively repeated?

- Is it not the intuition that feeds the imaginative conjectures, the analyst's alpha dream work, the ideograms that inspire interpretation?
- Would tolerance of chaos and turbulence of a very primitive quality, like what we experience since our primordial times, contribute to allow and enrich "intuitive capacity and intuitive health"?

(Cogitations. London Karnack books)

Their hypothesis seems to be an expressive and fruitful field for intuition and perhaps a precondition for it to emerge. In our profession, we have the privilege and opportunity to access primitive, intuitive and embrionary areas, which, as Bion says, may be buried in the future that has not happened or in the past that is forgotten, and which can hardly be said to belong to what we call "thought".

Teresa Rocha Leite Haudenschild, after focusing on the different models of child analysis, presents a clinical process from Bion's perspective. Her conclusion is that the analyst, by using his alpha function in a state of *reverie*, operates as an empathetic container for the protosensorial and protomental states of the analysand, in *unison* with the nature of their pain and emotions, "being with" and "dreaming" them (transformations in O). He may then propose some knowledge (transformation in K), and, based on the analysand's responses, modulate the analytical dialogue towards psychic growth. Given the almost total absence of verbal communication, intuition was fundamental to listening and the analytical dialogue. In her chapter she remarks that the introjection of containment is more important than the introjection of the internal representation of emotional contents, although both occur concomitantly. It is based on this introjection that the subject has a notion that there is an inner psychical space, an internal world, just as the object has, and these are unique.

Alicia Beatriz Dorado de Lisondo and Silvia Neborak in their chapter on infant observation with the Esther Bick method, underline Bion's observation theory as one of the goals of intuition for the emerging emotions in the bond so as to avoid unnecessary pain. By sharing the baby's life on a weekly basis with her multiple relationships, the observer makes imaginative and rational conjectures in creative ways: they are an invitation to develop her/his ability for intuition. She/he conquers a broader horizon that favors contact with her/his own primitive preverbal mental states. If this contact is tolerated, self-knowledge may become a compass for exploring "the baby parts" of patients.

Bion argues that the effective interpretation should bridge the gap between knowledge learned and truth lived. Within the context of this gap between reality and unreality he contends that "The interpretation must do more than increase knowledge" and asks, "Is it possible through Psychoanalytic interpretation to effect a transition from knowing the phenomena of the real self to being the real self?". Interpretations that simply increase knowledge maintain "the inaccessibility of "O", and "postpone 'O' indefinitely" (1965, pp. 147–149). From this perspective, accumulations of empirical knowledge function to occlude truth. Clinically, the analyst can offer interpretations that are true to the facts but that block the unfolding at-one-ment with the ultimate emotional truth of the patient: effective and accurate interpretations result in transformations in O (ultimate reality, truth) not simply in K (knowledge). They require a capacity for "at-one-ment" in the analyst.

Through the experience of the psychotic field in a large group, Guelfo Margherita, Alexandre Patouillard, Federico Pone, Salvatore Rotondi, and Loredana Vecchi observe a thought structuring, without dissolving the field, that can be brought to the formulation of scientific hypothesis; individuating therefore the point of observation from which can be perceived the co-presence, separated but deeply correlated, of experiencing the vital emotions of the field (container) and constructing the hypothesis swimming within it (contents). It starts a glimpse to the separation of the *two modalities of being*: asymmetric, information, rationality, scientific method and language of *interpretation*; and symmetric, entropy, irrationality, of oneiric, poetic, psychotic language, of *intuition* according to Matte Blanco's terms. In regard to understanding how communication is structured within and between the two levels the authors present clinical material.

References

Bion, F. (1997). *War memoires*, 1917–1919. Ed. F. Bion. London: Karnac.

Bion, W.R. (1940). The "War of Nerves": Civilian Reaction, Morale and Prophylaxis. In E. Miller (Ed.), *Neuroses in War*. New York: Macmillan & Co., 1945, pp. 180–200.

Bion, W.R. (1962b). *Learning from Experience*. Seven Servants. New York, Jason Aronson, 1977.

Bion, W.R. (1963). *Elements of Psycho-Analysis*. London: Heinemann.

Bion, W.R. (1965). *Transformations*. London: Heinemann.

Bion, (1967b). Notes on Memory and desire.

Bion, W.R. (1970). *Attention and Interpretation*. London: Heinemann.

Bion, W.R. (1979). Making the Best of a Bad Job. In *Clinical Seminars and Other Works*. London: Karnac Books, 1994, pp. 321–331.

Bion, W.R. (1992). *Cogitations*. London: Karnac Books.

Brown, L.J. (2019). *Transformational Processes in Clinical Psychoanalysis: Dreaming, Motions and the Present Moment*. New York: Routledge.

Grimalt, A. (2006). Transformació de l'experiència emocional. *Revista Catalana de Psicoanálisi*, XXIII(1–2).

Chapter 1

Negation as a method for intuiting psychoanalytic discoveries

Bion's turning point in "notes on memory and desire"

Ilan Bernat

Bion's (1967a) paper, "Notes on Memory and Desire", is considered by many to be a turning point in his theoretical and clinical thought, separating the "early" and "late" Bion. Through this paper and several other related notions, Bion has explicitly developed a method of negation designed to free psychoanalytic observation from its reliance on sensory and conceptual-verbal faculties, as almost exclusive means for grasping mental reality. Bion's method involves constant efforts by the analyst's consciousness to negate its reliance on these faculties, to "make room" for intuition.

In a way, Bion's method is an expansion of one of the meanings of Freud's (1925) notion of negation, referring to the function of judgment. In Freud's model, negating the sensory perception of the external object is required for the establishment of internal representations. This notion of negation echoes Freud's letter to Lou Andreas – Salome in which he described his experience when writing:

> I know that in writing I have to blind myself artificially in order to focus all the light on one dark spot, renouncing cohesion, harmony, rhetoric and every-thing which you call symbolic, frightened as I am by the experience that any such claim or expectation involves the danger of distorting the matter under investigation, even though it may embellish it. Then you come along and add what is missing, build upon it, putting what has been isolated back into its proper context.
>
> (Freud, 1916, p. 312)

Bion quoted this paragraph on various occasions, perhaps because Freud is emphasizing here – more than in any other reference – the negation not only of the sensory perception system but also of all secondary process functions in the conscious mind. This experiential description nevertheless contradicts Freud's (1911) metapsychology, which gives almost exclusive primacy to the conscious mind, with its sensory and verbal capacities to grasp reality.

In formulating the method of negation, Bion also drew on Bergson's (1896) distinction between utilitarian intellect and intuition. Bergson points out the effort needed to negate the utilitarian intellect that controls consciousness, to purge

DOI: 10.4324/9781003293385-2

perception of the automatic tendencies of inference and to enable the function of intuition, which is the only faculty that can perceive the essence of things (Torres, 2013).

Another source of inspiration for Bion's method is Negative Theology (apophasis). Mawson (2014) quotes from the Ascent of Mount Carmel written by 16th-century monk, St. John of the Cross, the demand for abandoning "memory in all its forms", including the five senses, in order to attain unity with God. This influence is reflected in the paper's religious structure and style. It begins with some postulates about memory and desire, follows with positive and negative commandments and concludes with consolation for those who adhere to these commandments. It reminds Momigliano (1981) of the Jewish *Shemah* prayer.

Important as these theoretical and philosophical sources may be, Bion's method of negation is above all based on his clinical experience. One should especially note the clinical examples he gave at various seminars (Bion, 1967b) throughout the year he spent writing this paper, to understand the experiences that gave rise to his theoretical thinking. Bion mentions these experiences as essentially "indescribable" (85) and "going off the end of the spectrum" (60). These patients bear a psychic pain so intense that it cannot be put into words; it remains buried deep within the mind as an indecipherable, unexperienced and unrepresented essence, which they are thus unable to express.

A few years before the "Notes", Bion (1962) saw the conscious and the unconscious as working in harmonious collaboration. First there is the conscious perception of information coming from the patient via the senses and language; then, this data is transformed into unconscious material in order to create what Bion termed "binocular vision". The turning point in his thinking occurred when he discovered that the transformations occurring in the session are much faster than the cognitive ability designed to perceive them. They occur, at the "speed of thought" (Bion, 1967c, p. 166) – the psychological equivalent of the speed of the light. Hence his conclusion that in these cases, conscious perception, which is designed to serve our daily needs, interferes with intuition – our more precise unconscious perception, capable of perceiving mental changes. Therefore, the negation of consciousness should be radical and occur right from the start, in the very formation of clinical facts.

Clinical implications

I suggest four clinical aspects of this negation method, which posits intuition at the center of the clinical encounter:

Tuning the mind

Bion (1965) referred to this 'tuned' consciousness as "a sort of positive lack of anything in one's mind" (13), a kind of empty consciousness. The thought exercise he proposed involved thinking about "the patient you are going to see tomorrow" (7). This sort of negative thought exercise resembles a Zen Kōan, as the patient who will arrive tomorrow is a non-existent entity. Any attempt to grasp it traps us in rigid memories, as the patient (and the analyst as well) has already changed since the previous session.

Evolution precedes interpretation

Bion shifts the key role of interpretation in classical psychoanalysis towards intuiting evolution. Interpretation is the verbal expression of what is revealed through extensive intuitive listening to evolution. The place from which one offers the interpretation is a depressive position. Still, this revelation is short-lived and made possible only by negation, by immersing oneself once again in the confusion and senselessness of the paranoid-schizoid position. According to Bion: "if one can be patient enough, one will see a pattern in this stuff which is turning up" (Bion, 1967b, p. 14). The notion of "being patient" captures in a unified manner the patience, the suffering, and the patient. Intuiting evolution is thus an often-unsettling emotional journey towards interpretation, which entails unconscious psychic work and requires the analytic pair to oscillate between positions.

Clinical vignette: Lily

Early on in Lily's therapy, I began confusing her name with similar-sounding names, occasionally using these out loud, without even noticing that I was doing so. Sadly, for both of us, this would sometimes happen during the more intimate moments of therapy. When I thought about what was happening, I felt that I disliked her name for some reason and that I was using an alternative that I found more personal. This was so even though her name was rather common and had evoked no resistance in me beforehand. Every time I called her by the wrong name, it would hurt her, causing a crisis in therapy to the extent that she nearly decided to terminate. She was certain that I was doing this on purpose. Besides sharing her pain, all I could say during those weeks was that I still did not understand what was happening to me, but that I believed that I would eventually. One day, after another session ended in this painful manner, I had the clear feeling of having 'grasped' what it was about, though I was still unable to formulate for myself what exactly was taking place. Without knowing much about her past, I felt that she was an un-held child, as if no one had even named her. In our next session, I asked her if she knew how or why she was given that particular name. In tears, she said that she never liked her name and that, as a girl, she had even thought about changing it, as she found it vulgar. Then, she told me that her mother had oddly chosen to name her after one of her favorite cosmetic products. We were both silent and sad about this empty and impersonal choice her mother made in naming her. There was no need to say anything more. I felt that now I could love her with the name she had been given and no longer altered it unawares.

In this case, negation involved the rejection of the quick explanations that came to mind as well as waiting and letting things grow inside me while having faith that they are on their way. For example, right from the start, Lily developed intense love-transference and, though I considered many times the possibility that I was reacting with negative counter-transference, it was not enough to convince me. Later on, in this period, the image of another patient with the same name that I had treated years before came to mind – it was difficult for me to like her as she had an air of neglect and carelessness and often engaged in indiscriminate sex. I had to let this foreign image develop inside me to perceive that a certain aspect of neglect that I found difficult to bear; was also present in my current patient. This eventually led me to the intuitive grasping of the deep connection between her name and maternal neglect.

I believe that Lily felt the relative calm I had maintained, and this made it possible to hold the situation. My question about how she was named was, in fact, an interpretation that stemmed from an evolution that happened inside me and only had to be pointed out, although I did not know what the answer would be.

Bion's clinical vignette

At one of his 1967 Los Angeles seminars, Bion (1967b) talks about a schizophrenic patient whose speech was so incoherent throughout analysis that Bion was constantly on the verge of falling asleep. Bion's attention suddenly woke up in one session, when the patient began telling him a dream: in his dream, the patient and his children were walking along a riverbank. All of a sudden, his children fell into the river and the strong current washed them away. The patient jumped in to save his children and was carried away with them to where the water vanished underground. "I can tell you", he says to Bion, "I never woke up so quickly in my life" (56).

After recounting the dream, the patient completely passed out, lying speechless and inert. Bion, to my mind, finding it hard to bear this sudden change, responds by saying, in a somewhat rude and detached manner, that it seems he did not wake up fast enough. The patient simply reverted to his regular incoherence and Bion concludes this vignette with words that express profound frustration: "that was that".

It was clear to Bion that the telling of the dream was one of the most significant and precious moments in the entire analysis, but there was nothing he could do to make this more present. The rare moment became a missed opportunity. Bion shares this with his audience without offering – or requesting – any explanation for what had happened.

Reading this description, I was astounded to recall the words Bion (1992) wrote in his diary, *Cogitations*, some eleven years later. Now at the end of his life, the words that the patient had said at the end of the dream came back to him and Bion asks himself if it was not him, the analyst, who was "too 'wide' awake, too conscious, too rational" (366). And he continues:

what sights did the patient see that made him 'wake up' so fast that he could not be swept down the stream? Was it the danger of becoming, like me, too wide awake? Or, like me, too fast asleep – in fact, the sleep of death?

(p. 366)

Bion writes this shortly before the anniversary of the battle of Amiens, which he took part in during World War I, sixty years earlier- the very day that he later said he had died on (Bion, 1982, p. 265). In his memoirs (Bion, 1982, pp. 121–141; Bion, 1997, pp. 22–38), Bion tells about watching soldiers drown in the Steenbeck river where he fought, and how, for many years after the war, as a student, he would wake up drenched in sweat from a terrible nightmare in which he saw himself sliding down a slippery slope into the gushing and muddy river (Bion, 1985, p. 16).

This painful example shows how the evolution of the patient depends on the evolution of the analyst. It was only negation that made it possible to carry this crucial and misunderstood analytic moment for years on end. When negation is possible, evolution can last a lifetime, even long after the end of analysis.

Moving towards at-one-ment with the patient's emotional reality

In the "Notes", Bion states: "Awareness of the sensuous accompaniments of emotional experience are a hindrance to the psychoanalyst's intuition of the reality with which he must be at one" (Bion, 1967a, p. 136). In this statement Bion presents a radical view that contradicts mainstream approaches, which emphasize the communicational and bodily aspects of emotion. Instead, the essential element of emotions is their existence as an individual's 'experience' – which is inherently silent and lies within the confines of the individual. The emotions of the other subject are transcendent essences; they do not really "come through" or are transmitted to us the way sense impressions do, nor are we at all capable of transmitting them to another person without undergoing a transformation which changes their original state. Bion goes a step further beyond language – not only language is barely able to get across emotional essences, the very expression of emotions – like language – does little justice to emotional truth and may even altogether blur it.

The work of negation the analyst must do, may be the most difficult task of all, while facing the outpour of the patient's expressed emotion due to the immense influence its presence exerts on the therapist's thinking and judgment. Instead of emphasizing the working through of sensory messages that are transmitted from the patient to the therapist, Bion stresses the movement taking place **inside** the therapist, who tries to include the patient's emotional reality in himself and be at one with it.

The notion of "being at one" is closely tied to the two main concepts in the paper "Intuition and Evolution", which should be considered as a single frame of reference for the kind of consciousness that the negation method seeks to enable. Bion later formulates this aspect as his notion of "O":

> I use O to represent this central feature of every situation that the psycho-analyst has to meet. With this he must be at one, with the evolution of this he must identify so that he can formulate it in an interpretation.
>
> (Bion, 1970, p. 89)

Clinical vignette: Ohad

Ohad came to analysis due to psychotic anxieties which led him to completely avoid sexual relations for many years. Ohad's mother had been reluctant to touch him, for fear of catching a disease, and was unable to take care of him during the first year of his life.

In the fifth year of analysis, Ohad was going through a divorce and his anxieties about beginning a new relationship led to him being acutely overwhelmed with emotion. He started arriving late to his sessions and during sessions would suddenly fall asleep for extended periods of time. While falling asleep, he would mumble incoherently and appear to be dreaming. He described these moments of "dreaming" as "a blank page" or as "thoughts emerging and fading", without being able to hold on to and pursue a given line of thought. He said that, in the sessions, he was unsuccessfully trying to dream of a woman-figure to which he could feel close. This state of affairs went on for several months. Ohad's frustration with the lack of progress made in analysis was enormous. He often complained that I was not doing enough to help him, that I should have said more during the session or woken him up as soon as he fell asleep. I felt that I was beginning to identify with his complaints and accuse myself of becoming indifferent and being unable to hold this situation sufficiently.

I then had the following dream: During our session, Ohad was in acute distress and asked me to touch him. I consider reaching my hand out to him but am hesitant. After the session, I consult with other professionals, and they all tell me that I definitely should have granted his request. I feel intense remorse for hesitating, and I conceive of my reluctance to respond to his request for touch as an act of cruelty.

At first, the dream seemed to me to be about my guilt – my inability to make it easier for him to bear his emotional overload – and the accompanying notes of seduction and transgression of boundaries. As I kept thinking about my dream, however, I noticed that I kept coming back to the great loneliness I felt at what I experienced as the criticism of my colleagues. I was surprised that the dream suggested that they sanctioned physical touch. When I contemplated this, it occurred to me that the acute abnormality and guilt I felt were perhaps resonating an unconscious part of the mother, who avoided any physical contact with Ohad. I now imagined her not as an absent mother but as a tormented and lonely woman, trapped within her strange fear of touch. I wondered whether she felt a ruthless guilt for not being able to devote herself to his care. As I stayed with this feeling, guilt gave way to a feeling of sadness. I remembered that Ohad told me that he was named after his mother's brother who died in an accident, when the mother was pregnant with Ohad. She became depressed for a long time. I felt sad for her and for Ohad and for her precluded motherhood. I felt that, for him, I was now this mother, who now can bear the sadness she could not have borne before. I became more able to accept my inability to relieve his pain.

In the following sessions, Ohad kept voicing his frustration with the analysis. He said that he was "coming in empty and leaving empty" and suggested decreasing the frequency of our sessions. When I listened to what he was saying, I noticed a change in the way I was taking it in: I no longer felt guilt and self-criticism at my limitations, but grief for the suffering he had to endure, alongside a renewed sense of significance regarding our work in analysis. I told him that I knew he was making a very big effort in analysis now, and that even though his labors seem fruitless at the moment, I believe that what is happening is important. What I said was not entirely unfamiliar to him, but I think that my voice carried the fortitude of our relationship and the faith I had in it. Ohad responded that he would like to explore the 'dark places' of his psyche and do the work that still needed doing.

The next months in analysis were fraught with much anxiety, but the impasse was behind us. Ohad shared a dream-like hallucination that came to him as he was taking a shower. He had a vision of a public shower stall that was amazingly beautiful, all in shades of blue and black. He felt something cold and alienated that brought up an emotional memory of the emptiness and loneliness that accompanied his childhood. He sensed that the shower was a frightening representation of a woman-figure. I thought that this was the first time he had been able to provide this mother/woman-figure with a representation – one that was seductive and threatening, an emblem of emotional absence, that he could now observe and think. Sometime later, he recalled the rare moments when his mother would wipe off his back after bathing or brought him a tub full of hot water for his feet on cold winter days. This time, these sensory memories were accompanied by feelings of concern on the part of the mother. This evolution of the mother-figure at the end of this period in analysis, enable Ohad to develop a sexual and emotional relationship with a woman, for the first time in many years. It seems that the annihilating power of the mother's absence had buried under it areas of care and concern. Momentary and partial as they were, they registered in Ohad's psyche but had remained inaccessible to experience and communication.

The change that took place in his relationships with women turned out to be fundamental and relatively stable. Still, our work concerning his experience of emptiness and its resulting anxieties went on long after that. As the years went by, Ohad developed a unique hobby: astrophotography. He explained to me how hard it was to capture celestial bodies with a regular camera in total darkness by using long exposure. In one of the sessions, he gladly showed me one of the pictures he managed to take after a long night of trying. It was a distant gas nebula, but its colors were bright and shining and the image lives on in my mind, as lively as if I had just seen it. I thought that, in his own way, Ohad was showing me the evolution of his internal mother-figure: the light of maternal presence may be feeble, but the prolonged exposure to it in analysis has left an invaluable and indelible cumulative impression.

Creating a bond of unity by using reverie

In his paper, "Notes on Memory and Desire", Bion links evolution to the notion of dreaming he developed earlier. He depicts evolution as follows: "It shares with dreams the quality of being wholly present or unaccountably and suddenly absent. This evolution is what the psychoanalyst must be ready to interpret" (Bion, 1967a, p. 137).

Dreaming is the conscious presentation through which we come in contact with evolution. However, this dream-like quality is also a characteristic of intuition, as it involves the activity of the α-function, which seeks to endow psychic reality with meaning, through reverie. Commenting on the subject of unity in the earlier citation, Ogden (2015) suggested viewing the analyst's self-renunciation as the precondition for reverie and for creating a shared psychological space of intuition.

I consider this shared intuitive space of reverie (or wakeful dreaming) as the aspect of unity in the patient-analyst relationship. It is a mutual connection between one unconscious and another, a connection of receptive wandering which is unrelated to an object. It sometimes takes place as a quiet progression, before intuition is anchored and lingers on the image that arises through evolution; sometimes, it may take on a more tumultuous quality, as in Ohad's case. Grotstein uses the term 'contingent reverie' to describe the kind of reverie the analyst engages in when treating "castaway patients", a reverie in which one cannot distinguish transference from countertransference. (Grotstein, 2010, p. 25).

In Bion's clinical accounts, negating one's conscious awareness is the key to enabling a relationship of shared, unified dreaming with the patient. In a note dated to August 4th, 1959, he states that:

> the analyst, identifying himself with the patient, feels the experience the patient is having, would be more understandable if the patient were asleep and dreaming . . . if the analyst were feeling what the patient seems to be feeling, then he the analyst, would be disposed to say, "I must have been dreaming".
>
> (Bion, 1992, p. 51)

Reverie is a unique kind of attention in which conscious awareness is negated and consigned to the background. But it is no less, in its essence, always a state of relatedness (Sandler, 2005, p. 646). The mother who is in the dream-like state of reverie is not disconnected from the reality of the baby she is with; quite the contrary, her reverie increases her receptiveness to the baby's mood and her capacity to take in its undigested psychic material, through her intuitive identification with it. Bion views the element of unity in reverie as the critical factor that enables the development of thinking. He states:

> As the analyst treating an adult patient, I can be conscious of something of which the patient is not conscious. Similarly, the mother can discern a state of mind in her infant before the infant can be conscious of it, as, for example, when the baby shows signs of needing food before it is properly aware of it. In this imaginary situation the need for the breast is a feeling and that feeling itself is a bad breast. . . . Sooner or later the "wanted" breast is felt as an "idea of a breast missing" and not as a bad breast present.
>
> (Bion, 1962, p. 34)

In the same vein as Winnicott's notion of the role of the mother at this stage, Bion also holds that the aspect of time is crucial. It is only through the mother's unique ability to use reverie to know her baby's needs even before it does, that she can offer the sufficient support the baby requires for tolerating the frustration of the need for the breast (the "bad breast"), a feeling that is without any representation, and transforming it into the representation of an absent breast ("no breast").

In *Cogitations*, Bion argues that the psychotic patient waits for the session as a place to dream in, as the session provides him with the support required for dreaming (Bion, 1992, p. 37). In my view, this notion offers the potential for achieving representations and psychoanalytic discoveries in the clinical setting – not through interpretation, but through the experience of a supportive analytic presence. The aspect of unity in reverie increases and broadens the range of our receptiveness to include subliminal messages from the patient, which are then transformed into α-elements; this unity also enables the development of a representation of absence which was hitherto impossible.

Clinical vignette: Efrat

Efrat, a young woman, came to me for analysis, several years after suffering a psychotic episode. The principal content of this episode was that she was giving birth to herself. In analysis, we concentrated on working through the psychotic material in her psyche, mainly through dreaming. I will describe a particular moment that took place about three years into the analysis. At this point, Efrat had gotten married and was beginning to contemplate having a child. This prospect, however, evoked in her a strong anxiety about motherhood and reminded her of her psychosis to the extent that she was considering giving up her desire for a child. More than any other stage in analysis, it was this enlivening of her memories of the episode that caused me to feel inside myself the absence of the mother as a live and active element in her psyche. It was accompanied by an experience of great sadness for a child in whom no-one took any joy and for the injury this inflicted on her psyche. I shared with her these insights, which she had so far denied quite markedly. She said that it was very difficult for her to talk about it and that we were touching things that had no form. Her fear of another breakdown was present in the analysis.

As we delved into this material, split-off feelings of early neglect and sadness that were never externally visible, began to surface. Efrat said she never thought of herself as having been such a sad child. In the sessions, her speech became vague and less intelligible, but I made no mention of that and simply waited. In one of the sessions, she said something along the lines of "I'm talking about children, it hasn't been born yet. How can you talk about no children?" Alongside her vagueness, I felt that her words had the clear and painful quality of dream-thoughts. At a certain point, she said, "I feel like I'm starting to talk about something, then bah. . . . It makes no sense. My thinking is disorganized. All in splinters. It reminds me of the psychosis, all kinds of splinters". I sensed that we were in a gentle and fragile moment of touching an emotional truth, a moment in which language collapsed. Still, at the very moment when she spoke, I "saw" these "splinters" floating before my eyes, hovering around the room, as a kind of magical and benevolent presence, like something out of a fairy-tale. I felt we were having a unique, shared, and unspoken moment of unity. In retrospect, I believe that this was a rare moment in the analysis when transformation converged into an entire psychoanalytic discovery of the link between birth and falling apart, a moment in which a new self-sense of existence was born within her.

The significance of this change became apparent in the following sessions, in which Efrat mentioned that her experience of being erased and lost in her various relationships was fading away. Later on, this process led to her becoming pregnant, giving birth to a baby and having a good mothering experience. We were able to terminate the analysis within a year.

While this analysis took place several years ago, the experience of those floating "splinters" is still very much alive in me, imbuing Bion's words with potent meaning: "The evolving session is unmistakable, and the intuiting of it does not deteriorate" (Bion, 1967a, p. 138).

In this example, the ability to "be at one" was the result of the cumulative work of reverie, with its dream-like quality, within a relationship of unity that allowed us to contain this moment. I believe that without these elements, made possible by the negation method, I hardly could have seen the "splinters" Efrat mentioned as a sign of transformation rather than pathology.

Sustainable psychoanalytic discoveries are the result of a steady effort of *negation*, which enables the analyst's and the patient's continuous contact with the evolution – with the kind of emotional memory and experiential knowledge that is revealed intuitively.

References

Bergson, H. (1896). *Matter and Memory*. Mineola, NY: Dover Publication Inc., 2004.
Bion, W.R. (1962). *Learning from Experience*. London: Tavistock.

Bion, W.R. (1965). Memory and Desire. In C. Mawson (Ed.), *The Complete Works of W.R. Bion*. Vol. VI. London: Karnac Books, 2014.

Bion, W.R. (1967a). Notes on Memory and Desire. In J. Aguayo and B. Malin (Eds.), *Wilfred Bion: Los Angeles Seminars and Supervision*. London: Karnac Books, 2013, pp. 136–138. Originally published in *The Psychoanalytic Forum*, 2, No. 3 (Los Angeles, CA).

Bion, W.R. (1967b). *Wilfred Bion: Los Angeles Seminars and Supervision*. Ed. J. Aguayo and B. Malin. London: Karnac Books, 2013.

Bion, W.R. (1967c). Second Thoughts. In C. Mawson (Ed.), *The Complete Works of W.R. Bion*. Vol. VI. London: Karnac Books, 2014.

Bion, W.R. (1970). *Attention and Interpretation: A Scientific Approach to Insight in Psycho-Analysis and Groups*. London: Tavistock.

Bion, W.R. (1982). *The Long Weekend, 1897–1919: Part of a Life*. Abingdon, UK: Fleetwood Press.

Bion, W.R. (1985). *All My Sins Remembered: Another Part of Life and the Other Side of the Genius: Family Letters*. London: Karnac Books.

Bion, W.R. (1992). *Cogitations*. Ed. F. Bion. London: Karnac Books.

Bion, W.R. (1997). *War Memoirs, 1917–1919*. London: Karnac Books.

Freud, S. (1911). Formulations on the Two Principles of Mental Functioning. In *S.E.* Vol. XII. London: Hogarth Press, pp. 213–226.

Freud, S. (1916). Letter from Freud to Lou Andreas-Salomé, May 25, 1916. In E.L. Freud (Ed.), *Letters of Sigmund Freud 1873–1939*. London: Hogarth Press, 1961.

Freud, S. (1925). Negation. In *S.E.* Vol. XIX. London: Hogarth Press, pp. 235–243.

Grotstein, J.S. (2010). "Orphans of O": The Negative Therapeutic Reaction and the Longing for a Childhood that Never Was. In J.V. Buren and S. Alhanati (Eds.), *Primitive Mental States*. London: Routledge, pp. 8–30.

Mawson, C. (2014). Editor's Introduction to Bion's Memory and Desire. In *The Complete Works of W.R. Bion*. Vol. VI. London: Karnac Books.

Momigliano, L.N. (1981). Memory and Desire. *Rivista Di Psicoanalisi*, 27: 546–557.

Ogden, T.H. (2015). Intuiting the Truth of What's Happening: On Bion's Notes of Memory and Desire. *Psychoanalytic Quarterly*, 84: 285–306.

Sandler, P.C. (2005). *The Language of Bion: A Dictionary of Concepts*. London: Karnac.

Torres, N. (2013). Intuition and Ultimate Reality in Psychoanalysis: Bion's Implicit Use of Bergson and Whitehead's Notions. In N. Torres and R.D. Hinshelwood (Eds.), *Bion's Sources – The Shaping of His Paradigms*. London: Routledge.

Chapter 2

The hidden side of the moon

Understanding/misunderstanding. Bion, no memory, no desire

Antonio Pérez-Sánchez

> The far (hidden or dark) side of the moon. Tidal forces from Earth have slowed down the Moon's rotation to the point where the same side is always facing the Earth – a phenomenon called tidal locking. The other face, most of which is never visible from the Earth, is therefore called the "far side of the Moon".
>
> (Wikipedia)

Reading Bion

The way Bion expresses his thoughts lends to misunderstanding. Every mental phenomenon is subsidiary to being "seen", at least, from two sides. This paradigm would be the psychic seen from the conscious and the unconscious. Although we psychoanalysts deal fundamentally with the unconscious, the conscious also constitutes psychic reality, so this is a provisional split. This duality is also present in that every person is the container of a psychotic and a non-psychotic personality; or envy and gratitude as the opposite extremes of the same phenomenon; or the depressive position cannot be understood without the paranoid-schizoid position; or the known must leave an opening for the unknown. Bion usually emphasizes only one of the two aspects; if we take the metaphor of the moon, it would be the hidden side part, the most difficult to access, which should not mean that he ignores the visible part. Therefore, a literal reading of his work leads to misunderstanding, to a partial vision of the psyche. That is what this chapter is intended to show, devoting special attention to intuition and the precondition for its emergence: a state of mind without memory and desire.

To Ogden (2004), the confusion in understanding Bion lies in not distinguishing two stages in his work: the earlier Bion (represented by *Learning from Experience*) and the latter (expressed in *Attention and Interpretation*). The earlier tells us of the endless dialectical movement between obscurity and clarification, and of a progressive cycle between knowing and not knowing, while in the latter Bion recommends getting rid of everything learned from experience in order to be receptive to what we do not know. Ogden concludes that these are two completely different psychoanalytic conceptions, two vertices, although both are necessary in order to offer a stereoscopic view of psychic reality. I do not find this radical

DOI: 10.4324/9781003293385-3

division between the two positions convincing. In both, the primary psychoanalytic objective of confronting the unknown is present, although in the latter Bion emphasizes the unlearning (either of what we know of the patient or of what we have read of Bion's work), which does not necessarily mean eliminating it definitively.

An additional factor that may have contributed to the confusion in understanding Bion is his use of languages from different disciplines and background: from the most abstract (the mathematical, the philosophical) to the most concrete, mainly that linked to physiology (metaphors of the digestive processes or the dynamics of binocular vision), going through psychoanalytic language itself (Freudian and Kleinian) as well as artistic. And sometimes Bion gives a definition, especially when it comes to new terms, or in some of the ordinary language, but at other times he takes for granted the meaning of common words.

What is more, Bion's work differs, in style and depth, from that of his Seminars. The former is the result of intense and prolonged reflection for years, where he exposes a vision of the essentials of psychoanalysis: psychic reality as something distinctive, and especially of the vicissitudes and obstacles in achieving a suitable method to observe it. In my opinion, a considerable part of his work tries to solve this paradox: to avoid everything that is impregnated with the sensuous, because it saturates the "perception" of unconscious psychic reality, but at the same time accept the inevitability of the use of language, loaded with the sensuous, to express it. Hence also, the risk of confusion.

The other way of disseminating his ideas has been through the numerous seminars taught in the psychoanalytic world (15, according to Abel-Hirsch, 2019) in which he also includes his reflections on the clinical material provided by other analysts. On the one hand, he uses here the same procedure as in his books: to emphasize the unknown side of psychic reality, avoiding the known side; or pointing to one single side, assuming that the audience will take into account the unmentioned side. The dense, rigorous and concise language of his writings gives way to a more spontaneous oral style (later transcribed for publication) of the seminars. In the writings there is a strong discipline, the same that he recommends for analytical work, without concessions that distract from the essential, nor literary flourishes, and with hardly any quotes from other authors. However, in seminars, it would seem that he relaxes, forgets discipline and unleashes his wit and sense of humour, a procedure that is sometimes very illustrative of his thinking but which, if taken literally, is reductionist and can lead to confusion.

For example, in the Italian Seminars he says: "the greatest help that a psychoanalyst can receive does not come from his analyst, his supervisor, his teacher, or the books he has read, but from his patient" (Bion, 1977, p. 18). This is certainly part of the truth. But is it not also true that no one can hamper the analysis more than the same patient? There is a risk of idealizing the patient's collaboration, when actually, at least in part, the latter is opposed to knowing his psychic reality, as we learn from Freud (the concept of resistance), and from Bion himself: "Growth resistance is endo-psychic . . . and is associated with turbulence in the individual" (Bion, 1970, p. 36). Therefore, we must take into account the Bion from 1977, without forgetting the Bion from 1970.

Given these difficulties, any new publication on Bion fosters the expectation of clarifying his obscurities. Authors ranging from Grinberg (1975), to Nicola Abel-Hirsch, 2019 going through the various Bionian dictionaries (López Corvo, 2002; Sandler, 2005) just to mention the best known, have contributes to this. Upon returning to Bion, frustration is inevitable. We fall into the trap of "saturating" our understanding, rather than being "blinded" (or almost) at each reading (of a Bionian text) in order to allow a light to be shed, with the help of clinical situations, on what Bion said and what he did not. This would be an example of a Bionian stance. Contrary to what it seems, I do not dismiss the contributions of the previously mentioned authors; in fact, their reading opens up questions or discloses new aspects. But we must put them aside momentarily and then return to them later.

In short, Bion invites us to observe psychic object – which, to continue with the metaphor of the moon – I imagine to be round, from a certain angle ("vertex") that, at first, only allows us to see the front side. Therefore, in order to access the hidden side, we have to get around the visible one, which requires a complexity and variety of perceptive and expressive paths that are not easy to convey, and not easy for the reader to grasp. The metaphor of binocular vision used in several passages throughout his work (1950, 1962, 1965, 1970), is suitable for understanding the conjugation of the visualization of the hidden side of psychic reality, the most difficult to observe, with the visible one, which, according to my idea, should not be ignored. Both are necessary for a stereoscopic 'vision' of psychic reality.

With these considerations in mind, these are, in my opinion, some of the Bionian topics susceptible to misunderstanding:

- "*Thought arises in the absence of the object*". Will it not also be necessary to recognize the nature of the previous link with the object, so as later to experience the presence of its absence?
- The concept of *containment* and, associated with this, that of *reverie*. It is a common misunderstanding to take containment as a synonymous for "enduring" the pressure exerted by the patient. And as for the *reverie*, it is sometimes understood as an attitude of dreaming with the patient. Does this mean that we have to dispense with our conscious reflective capabilities?
- To assume that Bionian thought lacks psychoanalytic theoretical content. Indeed, many of the Bionian developments arise from the Kleinian theory. Such as projective identification, and the theory of positions, to name the two most relevant.
- Bion's ironic and anti-dogmatic style of the Seminars is attractive precisely because of its transgressive and innovative tone, but it sometimes lends itself to being confused with and "almost anything goes" type proposal.
- The interaction of Ps ↔ D positions understood literally is a state of mind without possibilities of change, as has already been pointed out (Britton,

2003; Pérez-Sánchez, 1997). Ps ↔D is not static, but dynamic. This means that Ps (1) ↔ D (1) is different from Ps (2) ↔ D (2) and this is different from Ps (n) ↔ D (n).

- We could also add the theme of the congress: *intuition*. Is it possible, for a psychoanalyst, to access psychic knowledge only with intuition, without the counterpart of rationality?
- And finally, closely linked to the latter, the analyst's attitude *"without memory or desire or understanding"*. Should the analyst empty himself and cancel for good all knowledge, of the patient and his method, in a definitive way in order for intuition to emerge? For reasons of space I will only deal with the last two.

Without memory or desire

Bion's recommendation to the analyst in dealing with the patient is well known: "without memory and without desire", and even "without understanding and without sensory perception". A literal reading of this text puts us in a state of present emptiness, which does not recognize the patient's history, nor that of his relationship with the analyst, nor future perspectives to which they both "aspire". We will have to review the Bionian texts in order to clarify these statements and correct the possible error I have been pointing out, that his emphasis on the hidden side does not imply denial of the visible side.

In *Learning from Experience*, Bion already points out his concern that what we know about the patient will hinder the acquisition of new knowledge, but he does not disregard it:

> The capacity to remember what the patient has said needs to be *allied* to a capacity for forgetting so that the fact that any session is a new session and therefore an unknown situation that must be psycho-analytically investigated is not obscured by an already over-plentiful fund of pre-and misconception.
> (1962, p. 39; italics original from the author).

To put it the other way round: although in order for each session to offer a new psychoanalytic situation the analyst must forget the known, however, it must also be linked to his ability to remember. And here is what can be remembered. "Yet the analyst needs all the knowledge of the patient and the discoveries and work of his predecessor". In other words, he needs to consolidate his basic work method and apply it to a specific patient" (Bion, 1962, p. 39). In other words, the analyst does not cancel out what he already knows about the patient, nor what he has learned from his teachers in order to have his own method of working. Although, later in his work, he will highlight the need to strip us of any previous knowledge so as not to hinder the new one to be discovered, it does not necessarily follow that the analyst has to mutilate his previous experience with the patient.

In the very short paper *Notes on Memory and Desire* he says: "The only point of importance in any session is the unknown" (Bion, 1967, p. 17). And for this to be possible the analyst must obey the following rules:

1   Do not remember past sessions. . . . Otherwise, the evolution of the session will not be observed.
2   To avoid any desire . . . for "cure" or even understanding.

(Bion, 1967, p. 18)

Fortunately, Bion then clarifies the ambiguity of the term *memory* pointed out by the analysts who discussed the text. He distinguishes between two types of phenomena. One, the normal "memory": "the ideas that are presented [in the mind] as a response to the deliberate and conscious attempt to remember". And another type he calls "evolution" which he defines as follows:

> The experience in which some ideas or pictorial impressions float in the mind, unbidden and as a whole. "Memory" . . . is an experience related mainly to sensuous impressions: "evolution" I regard as based on experience which has no sensuous background but is expressed in terms which are derived from sensuous experience. For example, I "see", meaning I "intuit through the medium of a visual impression".

(Bion, 1967, p. 19)

Here we see the paradox we referred to earlier: avoiding experiences based on the sensory world but using sensory language to express it. He then recalls Freud's procedure of being artificially blinded in his work in order to concentrate all the light on the dark zone, which allows Bion to "intuit a present 'evolution' and lay the foundations for future 'evolutions' The more firmly this is done, the *less* the psychoanalyst has to bother about remember" (Bion, 1967, p. 20). I have put the adverb "less" in italics to point out Bion's non-radical stance on remembering. "Less" does not mean anything at all.

As "evolution" is a word in common use, we also presuppose its usual sense, namely, a "series of successive states in the gradual change of something" (Moliner)[1] or "gradual development of something".[2] That is, the Bionian evolution must include the idea of successive mental states; from one moment to another in the session; and from one session to the next, and from one moment of the analytic process to another, if this is the case.

Bion seems to juggle, to perform almost magic tricks. After distinguishing between the two types of "memory", the word "intuition" is produced from up his sleeve. As no meaning is specified, we take it in its normal sense. If we go back to the dictionaries, in short, they say: the ability to perceive, anticipate and understand intimately, and instantaneously, without the need for conscious reasoning, the truth of a thing.

That is to say, if we avoid the memory of remembering and desire, we manage to leave the mind in a state devoid of the accompanying sensory elements, which will allow "intuition" to emerge. But is this form of knowledge sufficient, or should we presuppose the "visible" side of the object under study? Also, what are the sources of intuition? What are its foundations? I believe that we must avoid the suspicion that intuition comes about by infuse science. Is not the (unconscious) experience of the analyst in his or her relationship with the patient during the analytical process one of the main bases of intuition. Do we not need to verify this "knowledge" also through clinical, non-intuitive, data? In other words, we need to oscillate between intuition and sensory perception, as well as between intuition and rational thought; that is to say, to adopt the Bionian potion of binocular vision, already mentioned. Otherwise, the analyst runs the risk of building an "overvalued" knowledge based on his own beliefs (Britton, 2003).

According to Bion, "'Desire' should not be distinguished from 'memory', . . . the terms should represent one phenomenon which is a suffusion of both" so that "the 'memory' is the past tense of the 'desire', the 'anticipation' being the future tense" (Bion, 1967, p. 19). So, if desire becomes a primary element of psychic life, can we literally apply the Bionian recommendation to do without it? Is learning and growth possible without desire or memory? Can the baby build a link with the (good) object – and the patient with the analyst and vice versa – if he does not retain good experiences? Is growth possible if the good object is not desired and anticipated? I am aware that I am caricaturing the situation in order to draw attention to the risk I am pointing out.

One of the central themes of *Attention and Interpretation* (1970), apart from that of lying and perhaps linked to it, is the *opacity* of memory and desire for an adequate psychoanalytic observation. The main reason lies in the sensory background of both, which interferes with the observation of psychic reality. As the arguments in favour of this position are abundant (they occupy four chapters), aimed at illuminating the hidden face, and the one most taken into account, I will only remember some passages of them, and later stop at the moment at which I support my idea that Bion does not reject the "visible side". First of all, let's emphasize that Bion speaks of opacity, not of the definitive suppression of memory and desire. This is a nuance that if it is taken for granted radically modifies the reading of Bion's recommendation.

This discipline that Bion demands for himself as an analyst, not only fosters intuition, as we said, but now goes further and tells us that it increases the analyst's ability to exercise "acts of faith". Here we enter a slippery terrain, in which it is easy to slip into a position in which "faith", instead of being considered from a scientific vertex, is understood in the usual sense linked to the religious, to become a "belief", in this case of the Bionian theory, for example. Bion's reasons that follow try to discourage this temptation.

> An "act of faith" is peculiar to scientific procedure and must be distinguished from the religious meaning . . . it becomes *apprehensible when it can be represented in and by thought*. It must "evolve" before it can be apprehended and

it is apprehended when it is a thought just as the artist's O is apprehensible
when it has been transformed into a work of art.

(Bion, 1970, pp. 34–35)

I think this is one of the most illustrative passages of the complexity of Bionian
thought, and perhaps of the psychic reality that he tries to capture. Not only does
it speak of "faith" as something different from the religious, because it needs
thought, but it ends up connecting it with artistic activity. Then he continues to
discuss the validity of "scientific faith".

The "act of faith" has no association with memory or desire or sensation. It
has a relationship to thought analogous to the relationship of a priori knowledge to knowledge. . . . It does not by itself lead to knowledge 'about' something, but knowledge "about" something may be the outcome of a defence
against the consequences of an "act of faith". . . . An "act of faith" has as its
background something that is unconscious and unknown because it has not
happened. . . . Anxiety is "known" by its secondary qualities. Yet no one has
any doubt about anxiety or about "feeling" the reality, though what is felt is
sensations associated with anxiety and not anxiety itself. Similarly, no one
who denudes himself of memory and desire, and of all those elements of
sense impression ordinarily present, can have any doubt of the reality of the
psycho-analytical experience which remains *ineffable*.

Bion (1970, p. 35)

In order not to distort Bion's words too much, I thought it was appropriate to
quote him at length. There is a background, of non-knowledge and non-sensuous,
from which the knowledge of something will emerge, although for this to be possible, it is necessary to "sense" it. This can be done through language, in the
case of the psychoanalyst, or through artistic expression in the case of the artist. In short, what was ineffable, non-existent, insofar as it was not "perceived",
acquires existence, reality, through the inevitable use of senses. Depending on
how we understand the last sentence of the quotation, "if we denude ourselves of
memory and desire, we will recognize the reality of the psychoanalytic experience
that remains ineffable", it can lead us to a dead end. Stripped of the sensory, we
will grasp the ineffable of psychic reality, but then how do we make it sayable
so that it becomes a transmissible experience, which is ultimately the goal of
psychoanalysis?

One can understand the difficulty Bion has in declaring that the analytical experience is ineffable. I think this is the crucial crux of the matter. The ineffable is
what precedes the artistic work, until the artist materializes it. Ineffable is religious feeling, so that only faith can provide an outlet. Ineffable is also that which
precedes scientific knowledge. But psychoanalysis is not art, nor is it religion, and
it tries to approach science. A difficult task, if we want to maintain the specificity
of this discipline. That's what, in my opinion, Bion's work is about.

In order to support the scientific character of psychoanalysis, within its specificity, and to avoid "artistic" or "mystical" temptations, I would now like to quote one of the few passages in which Bion explicitly does not reject what I have been calling "the visible side", the verifiable and which gives consistency to the ineffable. Bion says:

> There is the possibility of suppressing one or all of these functions of memory, desire, understanding, and sense either together or in turn. Practice in suppression of these faculties may lead to an ability to suppress one or other according to need, so that suspension of one might enhance the effect of domination by the other in a manner analogous to the use of alternate eyes.
>
> (Bion, 1970, p. 44)

We see here a more flexible proposal. It is not about eradicating all memory, desire, etc., in a definitive way, but that these functions can be suspended alternately, also achieving an effect of strengthening the others, just like that produced by binocular vision.

Clinical material

As one advances in one's psychoanalytic practice, and continues to study Bion, one increasingly gets the impression that another factor making it difficult to understand his work is the considerable gap between his theoretical and clinical work. Except in his early writings collected in *Second Thoughts*, subsequent reference to clinical material is almost limited to the cases presented in his Seminars. Therefore, we miss more of his own clinical practice. So, it will be understood that it is not an easy task to provide clinical material to support Bion's ideas. Anyway, we have to try, and in my case in order to support my idea that opacity of memory and desire does not imply to abolish them definitively.

After several years of analysis, in the last session of the weekly four, Ms. A says that it has been difficult for her to come. She makes frequent breaks, something unusual because she normally speaks with ease.

"I don't know how to explain what is happening to me . . . it's hard for me". I had already observed other times this comment, with a vague idea of something defensive, but I didn't stop, waiting for her associations. Today, my intuition acquires more strength and I tell her: It is a way to curb her immediate experience, by passing it through the sieve of reason.

Smiling, she admits this.

> I was just thinking of something similar, following what we saw sessions ago. I always use camouflage, to avoid contact with myself. When I say that "I don't know how to explain things", like now, it's like I'm facing something new, about which I have no idea. . . . When you take a plane for the first time, you have some reference; you have seen it in movies or on TV. Even

with your first childbirth, you also know something through those media. . . .
When I talk to a friend who also does psychoanalysis four times a week, what
she tells me about it has nothing to do with what I do here. They are like two
worlds. . . . That's how I feel. I don't know how to describe what is inside me.

After a pause she refers to curiosity, as something important for learning and
growth, but she does not know how to deal with it.

Perhaps you mean, I say, that you do not use it for learning and growth. (My
feeling is that we are talking "around" the analysis, not about what is actually
happening.)

She goes on a little with her intellectual reflections. Then she is a few minutes
silence. Finally, I intervene: "If there is no camouflage, you are afraid that everything that can disturb you about yourself will be exposed".

After a tense silence, she admits that this must be so. She cannot explain the
tension, but it reminds her of a family scene:

> I am with my brothers and sisters. We have asked our mother about our
> grandparents. Our father walks in, and everyone, including our mother, stops
> talking. Someone turns on the TV, and its sound covers the tension. Actually,
> I had never asked my father about his parents.

This scene suddenly evokes (does it "evolve" in me?) a dream of years ago: *she
is lying on a bed and I am behind. We are watching the images being projected on
a white wall.* Through this dream we had understood the kind of communication
she uses in analysis, by "projecting" the stories of her life as if they were a film,
alien to her and me. In today's session, I talk about my memory of the dream in
order to understand how she talks about her "movies" as a resource that covers the
tension in the presence of a frightening analyst-father. She doesn't know if I will
accept everything she says spontaneously.

Ms. A remembers the dream well and adds:

> at home there was never a ban on what to talk about, although it was under-
> stood that, depending on what you said. it could be considered silly or unsuit-
> able. During the last years of his life, my father had a different attitude, even
> a certain sense of humour. And it is this image that I have always preferred to
> remember. . . . But now the other one came back, the tense one.

I say that these memories could help us to understand the tension she feels, but at
the same time they take us away from her present situation with me.

"But I don't know what it can be, I have no idea. . . . Yes, there is still tension. . . . But I don't know". (*Silence.*)

Thinking about the dream, her general curiosity, and her grandparents, in the
absence of her father, I say, "When you 'turn off' talking about your external life
(TV), there is silence and tension appears. Perhaps you are afraid your curiosity

will emerge, particularly regarding the analyst. You can't ask about me, or my parents".

> Patient: Yes. I anticipate that. I know that you are not going to answer me. . . . It is true that I hold myself back. . . . Although nobody has told me that I cannot ask questions. Actually, that also involves talking about myself.

Comments on the session

I think there are *two intuitive moments for the analyst* in this session. One, when the patient repeats that "she does not know how to explain what is happening to her". Now the idea of her defensive subterfuge to avoid spontaneity, and "camouflage it" with a detailed account of something in her life has become stronger to me. It was not an exercise of reflection that led me to attach special importance to that moment; it was a strong feeling, based on similar previous experiences with the patient, that imposed itself on me as something important. That is to say, an intuition.

The other moment of intuition is when she associates a memory of her family, which evokes in me her dream of a long time ago. In that dream we discovered the type of analytic communication consisting of talking in a dissociated way about her life through her projected stories. Again, her memory awakens in me another memory, a dream, which I have not gone looking for, but which emerges with force. So, the session shows how the analyst's 'remembering' emerges in the course of his 'evolution' in the session. The session also illustrates the understanding of the "here and now" in relation to the historical past, and the past of the analytic process.

Final remarks

Binocular perspective, "without memory no desire" and intuition

I hope to have shown that possible misunderstandings in the comprehension of intuition, and of the prior mental state "without memory or desire", may be due to not taking sufficiently into consideration a fundamental aspect of the Bionian vertex for approaching psychic reality: binocular vision.

Discipline ↔ open-mindedness in Bion

Probably underlying the question of "without memory or desire" is a tension present in all of Bion's work, between opposing factors that alternate, and which could basically be summarized as follows: on the one hand, a scientific attitude in which the observation of reality requires an attitude that is as unprejudiced as possible, so as not to distort the observable reality, and which requires an effort of discipline. Above all, taking into account the specificity of the reality observed by psychoanalysis.

As Neri points out (quoted by Nicola Abel-Hirsch, 2019, p. 9), it is conceivable that such an attitude could have its roots in the personal experience of a person educated at a particular time in the British Empire, and then as a soldier in his country's army in the midst of war, both of which promote the need for a disciplined attitude. A discipline that, although necessary, comes from an establishment that is sometimes oppressive for the development of the individual, against which one would have to rebel.

Hence, we must reconcile the rigorous Bion of his writings with the 'open' and somewhat irreverent of his seminars. In other words, rigorous discipline and openness to the new are in interaction and are also the basis of any scientific attitude. This is what underlies the topic "without memory or desire", as well as the rest of his work. Could we say that this double attitude, disciplined on the one hand (especially in his writings) and alternating with an irreverent openness (especially in his seminars) on the other, corresponds to the basic attitude of a binocular vision?

Clinical insufficiency in Bion's work?

The gap between Bion's theoretical developments and the scarce clinical material from his own experience, especially in the second part of his work, does it create a distance between theory and clinic, which is sometimes difficult to bridge, or that can be a source of confusion, or simplistic technical positions, or of the "almost anything goes" type.

Acknowledgements

I would like to express my thanks to H.B. Levine for his suggestions to the manuscript, which have allowed me to clarify important aspects of it.

Notes

1 M. Moliner (1979). *Diccionario de uso del español*. Madrid: Editorial Gredos.
2 Oxford Dictionary.

References

Abel-Hirsh, N. (2019). *Bion: 365 Quotes*. London: Routledge.
Bion, W.R. (1950). The imaginary Twin. In *Second Thoughts* London: Karnac.
Bion, W.R. (1962). *Learning from Experience*. 3rd ed. London: Karnac Books, 1991.
Bion, W.R. (1965). *Transformations*. London: Karnac Books, 1991.
Bion, W.R. (1967). Notes on Memory and Desire. In E.B. Spillius (Ed.), *Melanie Klein Today*. Vol. 2, 1988.
Bion, W.R. (1970). *Attention and Interpretation*. 3ª ed. London: Karnac Books, 1993.

Bion, W.R. (1977). Cesura. *Two papers: The Grid and Caesura*. London: Karnac Book.

Britton, R. (2003a). The Analyst's Intuition: Selected Fact or Over-evaluated Ideas? In *Belief and Imagination*. London: Routledge.

Britton, R. (2003b). Before and After the Depressive Position. In *Belief and Imagination*. London: Routledge.

Grinberg, L., et al. (1975). *Introduction to the Work of Bion Strathtay*. Clunie Press, rep. London: Karnac Books, 1986 (revised ed. *A New Introduction to the Work of Bion*. N.Y. Aronson, 1993).

López Corvo, R. (2002). *Diccionario de la obra de Wilfred R. Bion*. Madrid: Asociación Psicoanalítica de Madrid. Biblioteca Nueva.

Moliner. (1979). *Diccionario de uso del español*. Madrid: Editorial Gredos.

Ogden, T. (2004). An Introduction to the Reading of Bion. *The International Journal of Psychoanalysis*, 85: 285–300.

Pérez-Sánchez, A. (1997). *Análisis Terminable*. Valencia: Promolibro.

Sandler, P.C. (2005). *The language of Bion*. London: Karnac Book, Intuition, pp. 348–360.

Chapter 3

Group construction of intuition

Fusionality and tenderness

Ruby Mariela Mejia Maza

> If psychoanalytic intuition does not provide us with a field for pawing wild donkeys, where could we find a zoo that preserves the species?
>
> (Bion, 1975)

I believe that the crossing of a moment of unison (*at-one-ment*) – patient analyst – with strong sensory resonance and the appearance of the T factor hypothesized by Gaburri, in which the analyst's receptivity opens up to Tenderness with an "intuitive visceral" perception, could prelude the reverie as a function that allows us to start thinking:

> Tenderness aims to grasp the hidden, split and unknown dimensions of the child, of the patient, in this sense, in order to develop, it needs the tolerance of the unknown which we call negative capacity. This ability transforms and makes the primary impotence, *Highflosigkeit*, tolerable, experienceable, thanks to the meeting with an interlocutor (mother-analyst-father) who tolerates, in turn, the asymmetry and dependence to which the encounter with the other always exposes us.
>
> (Gaburri, 2007)

The purpose of this work is therefore to observe how experiences of fusionality and tenderness can favor the appearance of intuition through a group analysis experience within the analytic field model developed in Italian psychoanalysis.

Bion in fact in *The Tavistock Seminars* deals with the transmission for which the concepts of transference and countertransference or of transitional object are not sufficient:

> It is in this context that whoever observes the groups would have the opportunity to assist in part to this form of inheritance. . . . you could observe an idea that proceeds in a zigzag way through the group. We don't know where an idea comes from, nor do we know where it goes, but we can observe it *during*

DOI: 10.4324/9781003293385-4

the passage. This is where we return to the exercise of analysis and practice of group observation.

(Bion, 2005, pp. 23–24)

If Freud advised artificial blindness to penetrate darkness, Bion (1992) asserts that "the psychoanalyst must exercise his intuition in such a way that it is not harmed by the intrusion of memory, desire and understanding", which requires a permanent discipline to create through our negative abilities, our "uncertainty principle" (Bion, 1975), a mental space for "uncertainty, mystery and doubt" which is the mental state required to get in touch with O.

> The more the analyst succeeds in approaching a condition of freedom from these opacities – and certainly from other "opacities" not yet identified – the more confident he can assume that the origin of his observations is not due to his "personal equation".
>
> (Bion, 1992, p. 316)

In *Intuiting the truth of what happens* Ogden believes that Bion proposes in *Notes on memory and desire* a revisited analytical methodology in which he "supplants awareness from its central role in the analytical process and settles in its place the analyst's work (largely unconscious) to intuit the psychic reality (the truth) of the session by becoming one with it" (Ogden, 2016, p. 79). If for Bion, when the time comes when the analyst is ready to formulate an interpretation, the work has already been done, Ogden adds that

> the work has already been done, in the sense that analyst and patient have already been transformed by the experience of jointly sensing the disturbing reality with which they have become one, a previously unthinkable psychic reality that changes both the patient and the analyst. The interpretation is superfluous.
>
> (Ibid, p. 81)

Rêverie, the waking dream, is the paradigmatic clinical experience of the intuition of psychic reality.

The etymology of intuition derives from the Latin verb *intueri*, "looking inside", what we can do only with the mind's eye. As a metaphor for intuition, a self-portrait by Giacometti (1935) can be evoked in which the artist represents himself with an open eye that looks outwards and questions the world; the other closed eye is turned towards the inner cavity, intent on knowing and understanding his subjective perceptions. With Milton's words, intuition allows us to "see and tell/of things invisible to mortal sight". In moments of emotional intuition there is a conjunction of conscious and unconscious elements (Symington, 1996), intuition of the new fact preparatory to transformation and mental growth.

Intuition alludes to a moment of rupture, a sudden flash that leads us to an unexpected understanding that gives clarity to our vision, a form of non-rational knowledge that however depends on previous experiences in analogy with what happens in science. One of the staunchest supporters of the power of intuition was the illustrious mathematician Hadamard (1865–1963), who in an investigation into the practices followed by mathematicians observed that many important discoveries were preceded by periods of unconscious "incubation", followed by sudden lighting that was then subjected to verification. Influenced by his predecessor Poincaré (1854–1912), for whom science demonstrates what intuition discovers, he concluded that "The roots of creativity, both in science and the arts, do not lie in consciousness but in a long unconscious mental activity and in the unconscious aesthetic selection of ideas that subsequently enter consciousness "(cited by Eddi De Wolf, 2017, p. 16).

Corrao (1985) maintains that the prevailing logic in analysis is that of Abduction, a logic that Peirce added to the canonical ones of deduction and induction; it is a logic of hypotheses and of the sense in which "intuitive functions" prevail, in such a way as to displace the operation of thought from the level of bivalent logic towards that of analog or symmetric logic. The psychoanalytic field, comprising the analyst, the patient and theories, functions as a system of transformations activated by the shared interpretative function and by *koinodynia*, the experience of sharing pain in a group, which "makes it possible to reconstruct the verbal sense of pain and to relearn the original generative experience in finding the constant conjunction between words and things, between the multiple and the one, between the whole and the parts" (Corrao, 1986, p. 126).

A key concept is that of *Gamma Function* (Corrao, 1981) which is the analog in the group of the alpha function for the individual and is related to the polyadic structure of the multiple group spatial configurations. *Koinonia* includes the dimension of *togetherness*, of the *in-common*, and of the creative use of metaphor and analogical speech to make catastrophic changes and the transformation of unthinkable emotions into the capacity to *suffer pain* possible.

In group analysis, each individual transfers parts or aspects of his or her self to the group as a function of the mirroring phenomenon; in certain moments a real group *self* functions in the group as a result of both the projections of the individual selves of the members and the personification effect.

Group session

After more than three years from the beginning of the group analysis, conducted with two weekly sessions, after the summer holidays they greeted me with the doubt: "I still don't know if the doctor is good or bad". This led me to really ask myself about my "severity" and "abstinence" which, masked by rigor, could hide a persecutory or judgmental aspect of me. Target of evacuative projective identifications on disappointing and cold mothers, with an inability to trace their projections, I experience a loss of intuitive skills. Absorbed in countertransference I lose sight that my "badness" is probably due to their having missed the group and their sense of abandonment during the break.

Before the following session there was a violent storm and under the deafening bombardment of hail in the flooded city, I experienced moments of panic and helplessness, I feared that I would not be able to get to my consulting office. In addition, the session begins with a delay of 40 minutes due to the fact that we waited for the third participant stopped by the rain, it is our rule that the session is not held with two members. Rosanna arrives out of breath, each of them recalls the feelings of fear and danger experienced in crossing the city under the storm, with the underlying fear that the group would not meet and the concern for the leader's safety.

Rosanna says that furthermore the previous night she did not sleep, she had to take her father to the First Aid for a sudden pain, she feared the worst; she who is normally very reserved starts to cry recalling the fragility of the father who "no longer has the strength". They get in touch with her pain, listen to her with great emotional participation and share their own fears of losing their parents despite their ambivalence; Luisa talks about her ill father who has always been the child of the family cared for by both her mother and her. Gilda talks about her sacrifices to accompany her father, authoritarian and insensitive, in his chronic hospitalizations due to a tumor; despite her hostile feelings, his possible death inspires pity: "Your father will be grateful to you", she tells Rosanna.

They all have in common the fact that they come from families where they had to take care of the parental figures in a reversal of roles. I sadly remember my frail and sick father before his death. I wonder if the group is trying to deal with the anger caused by frustrated expectations of being saved and protected with a reciprocal of the dependency basic assumption by having to take care of me, they are concerned about my safety and the survival of the group.

Suddenly Rosanna stops and asks news of Beatrice, an absent member who has lived her pregnancy in the group and is now having a baby. I read the message in which Beatrice communicates that she gave birth with a cesarean and the newborn is fine. The group moves between empathy for the fears of death of the father and joy for the birth of the expected child.

Rosanna adds that in addition to the aging of her parents, it hurts her to reflect on her shortcomings, without a partner, without projects, for the first time speaks of non-vital dead parts in her; to my amazement Luisa, who joined the group a few months ago and is normally silent, delicately speaks to Rosanna of her depression, of her being anchored to the past for fear of losing good things and of the underlying anger and closure here too. Silence.

Gilda suddenly remembers a dream she made after the last session in which she finds herself with Manuela, her wedding witness, in her childhood home; the strange thing is that in her bedroom there was a tame Brown Bear. She is lying on the sofa and when she gets up she realizes that she is full of cat hair. The bear is closed, she says, as when we talked about Rosanna's closure.

Due to the functional regression that leads to transfer some individual functions including the alpha function to the group, it is activated a *gamma function* that allows transformative operations on the raw sensory and emotional elements present in the group field, generating dreamlike, mythical thoughts, etc. In fact, the figure of the "Bear", a dangerous animal that here magically appears "domesticated" in a familiar environment is an attempt to deal with their projected aggression and may be sexual drives (the cat hair) and their ambivalent dependency of the group that might not survive to their attacks.

Luisa associates the cartoon "Masha and the bear" (maybe evoking the therapist's surname Maza) I ask about it and they tell it animatedly. It is a pestiferous and orphaned Russian girl, with a bear, a parental figure that acts as "father and mother together" and solves all the problems; the atmosphere has become playful, everyone sees it, they recall different episodes that make them laugh, "doctor you must see it", they tell me in which channel I can follow it.

Gilda remembers that as a child she could play with cats only with gloves because of the fear of her parents, now she plays even without touching them, they understand everything; in the dream the sofa was full of cat hair, as she was too; the sofa was made of velvet, she makes the gesture of caressing it with her hands, the Bear is hairy.

I ask who is the Manuela of the dream? Gilda describes her as an older friend who has been like a mother to her, she always understood if she had something unlike the schizophrenic mother who did not understand her and never caressed her.

There is a moment of intense sadness and silence. I think of the difficulties previously expressed in analysis by Gilda in "touching", for her it was disturbing both to maintain eye contact and also to greet each other by shaking hands, as I normally do only before the holidays.

With sudden astonishment she remembers that once Manuela gave her Winnie the Pooh, a beautiful small teddy bear. They all follow this famous Disney cartoon in which the honey-loving character lives adventures in an imaginary forest with his friends, each of which represents a different mental disorder. It seems a group representation and now the members overlap telling episodes in a playful, joking, sweet participation.

Individual boundaries seem disappeared, and I feel wrapped up by a new sensation of intimacy and tenderness.

I emerge from this deep emotional involvement saying that our mutual waiting for both the newborn baby and the real expectation to start the group, having crossed the danger and feelings of fear and helplessness aroused by the storm (perhaps we have also saved a shipwrecked woman), the co-presence of birth and fear of death and being able to survive, the appearance of the bear/substitutive mother as a good object, allowed the group to get in touch in a new way, more willing to be "touched" by unexpected feelings such as tenderness.

The activation of the *gamma function* allows the group to come into contact with pain and O. An unconscious emotional experience that becomes conscious, a moment of unison, *at-one-ment*, a transformation in O that goes towards K but only *a posteriori*.

I am surprised at both the new aspects that each member of the group reports and the undifferentiated merger condition that underlies the relational field. In this regard, I subsequently found Neri's reflections on fusional containment and Gaburri's on T factor, tenderness, very pertinent.

The auditory, tactile, soft, contact sensations, the intimacy of the playful and rhythmic exchange, seem to dissolve the boundaries in a shapeless and enveloping skin, in the Fusionality, which takes on a containment function as Neri suggests:

> in the fusional containment there is the fantasy of flowing in a container capable of expanding almost to the infinite with which one becomes one, which protects from the risk of fragmentation and defends against external and internal stimuli. If the fusional incorporation has the effect of avoiding becoming aware of the other as an autonomous person, however "the object" can be loved (and in a very special way also known) only after it has been, fusionally, made its own.
>
> (Neri, 1990, p. 115)

Freud (1905) believed it necessary to integrate tenderness and passion into mature love, and Ferenczi (1949) stressed the confusion of languages that traumatically exposes the child to the language of adult sexuality, while Gaburri (2007) identifies in tenderness a precursor of the alpha function that it is located on the borderline between identification processes and movement towards the object.

Gaburri (2011) theorizes that if basic assumptions engulf the individual, tenderness "summons adults to listen to the child as different and unpredictable", it is the means that diversifies the passions of hate and love by transforming the undifferentiated condition into the normal affective ambivalence. If the analyst, differentiating himself from his sexual drive, succeeds in developing a receptive sensitivity to open a dialogue of tenderness with an "intuitive-visceral perception", a sort of protolanguage that allows, to put it in the words of Freud (1905), to "teach the child to learn to love" and, in Bion's words, to "learn to think". Tenderness not as a moving transport towards the patient's childhood traumatic vicissitudes nor as a push towards care; it is rather a listening and a look on the part of the analyst, attentive to grasp the internal, split thrust, which seeks a way to emerge from the network of primitive, contradictory, compliant identifications, in the basic assumptions in which patient got tangled up. The goal would be to create a space of potential acceptance of both the preconception of the breast and the preconception of separation. In this sense Gaburri conceives Tenderness as a precursor that prepares and nurtures the reverie that conveys confidence in emerging differences.

The appearance of tenderness in analysis, directed towards others or towards the parts in need of oneself from which one must separate, allows us to grasp aspects of the patient's self that were previously dissociated. The same need to receive tenderness makes us fear it and lays bare our needy, small and even greedy parts. It must be added that tenderness should not be sought, it occurs spontaneously in analysis when one has held a right position in the relationship and many different unions have been crossed (Neri, 2015).

The session that I am about to describe happens about a month and a half after the previous one and starts some 15 minutes later due, for the first time, to a delay of which I warned apologizing, and which caused me the anxiety of not being able to arrive.

There are four participants, and we are in the process of the Christmas holidays. Gilda talks about a chocolate cake sent to maternal relatives with whom she is recovering the relationships hitherto foreclosed by her father. I think it's my son's favorite cake; they talk about this cake, "the best Italian pastry"; someone has prepared a shrimp risotto, they are all hungry since we are near dinner time. Are they anxious about the imminent separation?

Furthermore, in the preceding session Gilda has announced that in two months she will leave the group for an individual analysis. When she initially arrived at the group, she asserted that she would have never done an individual analysis, she could not accept "to talk with a wall with someone behind her". She was also terrified about having a baby; even though for her group analytic training "requirements" she could have left the group after two years, it's only now, after almost four years of group analysis that she feels ready to start an individual analysis and to face more deeply her difficulties with motherhood.

Then Gilda remembers a dream with the Paddington bear that came from the "wonderful Peru" (country of origin of the therapist). Almost whispering she says that the bear was in search of a family to adopt him.

The figure of the Bear associated with the analyst reappears at a time when the imminent separation and fear of loss jeopardizes the dependency basic assumption; there is an attempt to deny the anger and aggression associated with frustration with a reversal movement, it is the bear analyst who is little and needs to be adopted. May be at an individual level symmetrically Gilda also refers to her silent desire of being adopted by the leader.

Everyone knows him, they laugh and joke. They say it is a little bear who had learned English; there is an earthquake, and they send him to England where he has to wait standing in a station until he finds a family to welcome him, in fact he will then be adopted.

In a subsequent dream Gilda found herself in front of three elevator doors, one large, one medium, one small, she did not know which one to choose. Beatrice exclaims "beautiful this of the three measures . . . as in fairy tales". I associate the story of Goldilocks and the three bears and they amusedly try to reconstruct the plot, the girl who enters a small house in the woods and finds a large, medium and small bed . . . this is too hard, this one is too soft, until she finds the right one, and so on with bowls and more . . . she enters the house when there are no bears, but they don't remember if the ending will be terrible or good. They all participate overlapping and time and individual identities seem to dissolve in the group.

Beatrice only now realizes that she will miss Gilda, it will certainly be a mourning. Silence. The joyful atmosphere gives way to sadness. Luisa rocks rhythmically in her chair, Gilda is almost lying on hers. Someone observes that the noise of the air conditioner brings to mind the fantasy of flying in an airplane or being in a kind of ship, moved by the undulating flow of the waves of the sea.

I feel that the fusional fantasy reappears, may be as a defense from fear and the loss feelings.

With a different and more reflective emotional tone Beatrice remembers a seemingly bloody ritual: in a primitive people when they had to face a mourning of loved ones, they were eaten to appropriate their qualities . . . it was sweet and tender in spite of everything, it was a way of preserving them. . . . Again, a reversal of violence in an attempt to reconcile the aggression aroused by abandonment with the feelings of need for love and containment. Silence.

They ask Beatrice about her mastitis and she replies that she is well now, the baby grows up, had some initial difficulties with breastfeeding and since he's big and eats a lot, she had to give an integration . . . but as soon as she caresses the baby and he feels her smell, he opens his mouth, she stands up and makes gestures to actively suck with the mouth open and moves the face as if looking for the nipple "I feel a breast that walks . . . before for me the breast was a sexual organ, now I am a breastfeeding breast . . . I spend the day with a bare breast and the other covered, always ready". It feels good when the baby is satisfied, she is sick if he is restless or hungry. Like a sudden flash both Rosanna and I exclaim "the Amazons!".

The image of Beatrice with one naked and one covered breast took shape in our minds in the sudden intuition of the image of the Amazons, the fighting women warriors who mutilated or uncovered their right breast to better carry their weapons. I can't help remembering Bion (1961) when he tells us that the individual's relationship with the group is as difficult as the infant's relationship with the breast. Fusion and tenderness seem to embody in an almost sensory way the emotional field of the group in a deep and emotionally engaging resonance that allows opening to states not accessible to consciousness, breast-group with which to merge but from which to also differentiate.

The various mythologemes present in the Greek myth condense the complex affective movements that lead to the preconception of the breast and separation.

To my amazement, only later did I discover that Gaburri (2011) evokes with regard to tenderness the myth of the duel between Achilles and Penthesilea, the queen of the Amazons who rushed to Troy to fight against the Achaean ranks.

The Greek hero at his birth was called "The Weeping" because his mother Theta, an immortal nymph, every day smeared him with ambrosia and every night she put him on hot embers in order to evaporate the mortal paternal part. When his father Peleus discovered the torture, he removed him from his mother to deliver him to the centaur Chiron who fed him with wild animals. So the boy changed his name and became Achilles: "the one who did not put his lips close to the breasts".

We know only of Penthesilea's childhood that she was beautiful and that she had been condemned by Aphrodite to know love only through rape. In fact, according to a version of the myth, Achilles wounded her in the right breast, but the last glance of the dying rider made Achilles fall in love, he was struck and raped her dead body. In the controversial version taken up by Heinrich von Kleist in 1808, it is Penthesilea who kills Achilles in the duel, and then, kidnapped by passion, she unravels him and devours him.

Both heroes, characterized by their undifferentiated and ambiguous sexuality, seem to have had a mirror childhood, in which Gaburri sees a paradigm of trauma resulting from a reversal of projective identification between adults and children; the lack of tenderness prevents the "realization" of the breast preconception. They lacked the experience of being welcomed and contained by a tenderly passionate breast, which can be touched, sucked, bitten, eaten, penetrated, by her baby. They can express their passion only through the violent or cannibalistic incorporation of the dead object, perhaps less dangerous because it is defenseless (without weapons), and not through introjection lacking the integration of tenderness and sensuality (Khan, 1973).

According to Bion (1963), myth is one of the learning tools of the primitive apparatus of the mind, a form of preconception waiting to find new meanings. The myth, Corrao highlights, contains an implicit model of mental functioning which thanks to its complex, polymorphic, polyvalent and polysemic structure reconnects the whole and the parts and favors new connections. The mythopoetic ability of the group through "field amplification" (Corrao, 1992) activates the narrative function and allows to transform emotions by widening gaze to wild and archaic elements previously unknown re-updated in the group experience.

Tenderness seems to keep opposites in balance, lays bare our frailties, accompanies moments of loss and mourning (La Torre and de Grazia, 2018). In fact, perhaps it is no coincidence that in both sessions the danger of the group's survival was crossed, there seems to be a conjunction of the shadow of death and vital generative elements.

Freud describes the tender love of the mother as bodily, physical, rhythmic, tactile; Neri (2015) recalls that Levinas associates respect and delicacy in approaching to each other with tenderness to caress. In fact, the feeling is that our minds in the group have really "touched" in a movement of mutual transformation. Gaburri (2008) imagines tenderness as a transformation of L (Love) towards O which allows the metabolism of both H (Hate) and K (Knowledge).

The difficulty in focusing the intuition conceptually led Bachelard (1966) to assert that "an intuition is not demonstrated, it is experienced". This seems to be in line with Bion's previously mentioned statement about the need to intuit unconscious psychic reality by becoming one with it. Intuition thus becomes the engine of mental growth (Bion, 1977), harbinger of new associative beginnings and creative transformations.

References

Bachelard, G. (1966). *L'intuition de l'Instant*. Paris: Gonthier.

Bion, W.R. (1961). *Experiences in Groups*. New York: Basic Books.

Bion, W.R. (1963). *Elements of Psychoanalysis*. London: Heinemann.

Bion, W.R. (1975). *A Memoir of the Future. Vol. I: 'The Dream'*. London: Karnac Books, 1991.

Bion, W.R. (1977). *Two Papers. The Grid and Caesura*. London: Karnac, 1989.

Bion, W.R. (1979). *A Memoir of the Future. 1: The Dream*. London: Karnac.

Bion, W.R. (1992). *Cogitations*. London: Karnac. [Bion, W.R. (1996). *Cogitations*. Pensieri. Roma, Armando].

Bion, W.R. (2005). *The Tavistock Seminars*. London: Routledge, 2018.

Corrao, F. (1981). Struttura poliadica e funzione gamma. In *Orme. Vol. II Contributo alla psicoanalisi di gruppo*. Milano: Raffaello Cortina, 1998, pp. 34–41.

Corrao, F. (1985). Il senso dell'analisi. Teoria e prassi dell'evento (Nota Seconda). In *Orme. Vol. II Contributo alla psicoanalisi di gruppo*. Milano: Raffaello Cortina, 1998, pp. 98–108.

Corrao, F. (1986). Il concetto di campo come modello teorico. In *Orme. Vol. II. Contributo alla psicoanalisi di gruppo*. Milano: Raffaello Cortina, 1998, pp. 115–129.

Corrao, F. (1992). *Modelli psicoanalitici. Mito Passione Memoria*. Bari: Laterza.

De Wolf, Eddi (2017). L'intuizione. In *Intuition*. Venezia: Palazzo Fortuny 13.05–26.11.2017 Catalogo, Fondazione Musei Civici di Venezia e Axel and May Vervoordt Foundation, pp. 13–26.

Ferenczi, S. (1949). Confusion of the Tongues Between the Adults and the Child. *International Journal of Psychoanalysis*, 30: 225–230.

Freud, S. (1905). Three Essays on Sexual Theory. In *S.E.* Vol. 4. London: Hogarth Press.

Gaburri, E. (2007). *Tenerezza e rêverie*. Milano: Centro di Psicoanalisi "Cesare Musatti".

Gaburri, E. (2008). Pulsione e funzione. In G. Corrente (a cura di), *Con Bion verso il futuro*. Roma: Borla, 2009.

Gaburri, E. (2011). *Mito, passione e tenerezza*. Venezia: Colloquio Italo Spagnolo.

Juliet, Ch. (1986). *Giacometti*, Universe Books, NewYork.

Kahn, M.R. (1973). Cannibalistic Tenderness in Nongenital Sensuality. *Contemporary Psychoanalysis*, 9: 294–302.

Kleist, H. (2008). *Pentesilea*. Venezia: Marsilio.

La Torre, D., and de Grazia, P. (2018). La Tenerezza. In *Koinos. Gruppo e Funzione Analitica*, anno VI, n. 2, pp. 137–150.

Neri, C. (1990). Contenimento fusionale e relazione contenitore-contenuto. In Neri C, Pallier L, Petacchi G, Soavi GC, Tagliacozzo R., *Fusionalità. Scritti di psicoanalisi clinica*. Roma, Borla.

Neri, C. (2015). La tenerezza e la capacità di relazione. In *Il fattore T in psicoanalisi. La tenerezza nel lavoro di Eugenio Gaburri (a cura di Granieri A.)*. Roma: Borla, pp. 26–36.

Neri, C., Pallier, L., Petacchi, G., Soavi, G.C., and Tagliacozzo, R. (1990). *Fusionalità. Scritti di psicoanalisi clinica*. Roma: Borla.

Ogden, T. (2016). *Reclaiming Unlived Life: Experiences in Psychoanalysis*. London and New York: Routledge.

Symington, J.E.N. (1996). *Il pensiero clinico di Bion*. Milano: Raffaello Cortina, 1998.

Symington, J.E.N. (2006). *A Healing Conversation: How Healing Happens*. London: Karnak.

Chapter 4

Intuition, memory and desire

Guido Berdini

Introduction

As is well known, Bion held that the analyst must maintain the discipline of suspending memory, desire and understanding. Coupled with the "act of faith", the negative capability's intrinsic abstinence creates the "conditions of possibility" for intuition to come into contact with the events that are evolutions of O.

But precisely which processes are traceable to memory and desire? I would like to suggest that during the course of a session, the analytic couple deals with numerous competing "configurations" waiting to be seen. Some of them, insofar as they are deeply steeped in pleasure or pain, are liable to impose themselves more quickly than others: the meanings they express are immediate, almost self-evident. Such facts would appear to bring us to the subject of hallucinosis, a mental state colonized by the sensuous dimension, by protosensations and by protoemotions that have yet to undergo an alphabetization. As Bion tells us, "[hallucinosis is] a state always present, but overlaid by other phenomena, which screen it. If the other phenomena can be moderated or suspended, hallucinosis becomes demonstrable" (Bion, 1970, p. 250).

In a condition of hallucinosis, meaning is totally different from that proper to rational thought. The mental event turns into sensuous impressions producing pleasure or pain; meaning is lost and is no longer available for exploration. For example, it could happen that a memory becomes so possessed by a "desire" belonging to a constellation of thought associated with feelings of "grievance, regret, or remorse" that mental growth is precluded (indeed, in this paper, I would like to examine some instances of this kind of possession as they occurred in a clinical case that I will present later). However, if the analyst is to come into contact with the patient's hallucinosis, (s)he cannot avoid abandoning his/her own personal hallucinosis sustained by memory and desire:

> it is necessary that the analyst undergoes in his own personality the transformation O → K. By eschewing memories, desires, and the operations of memory he can approach the domain of hallucinosis and of the "acts of faith" by which alone he can become at one with his patients' hallucinations and so effect transformations O → K.
>
> (Bion, 1970, p. 250)

DOI: 10.4324/9781003293385-5

Thus, the quest for meaning implies an unsaturated quality. Bion writes about how there is

> an evolution, namely, the coming together, by a sudden precipitating intuition, of a mass of apparently unrelated incoherent phenomena which are thereby given coherence and meaning not previously possessed (. . .) From the material the patient produces, there emerges, like the pattern from a kaleidoscope, a configuration which seems to belong not only to the situation unfolding, but to a number of others not previously seen to be connected and which it has not been designed to connect.
>
> (Bion, 1967b, p. 168)

Maintaining an empty and unsaturated state of mind allows a transformative 'space' to exist. One that can generate continuous crisscrossing references to meaning based on invariants. To this, the oscillating processes PS ↔ D, Container-Contained (♀ ♂) and Negative Capability ↔ Selected Fact all contribute.

Without prejudice to the specific role of the analyst, which necessarily embodies an ineliminable element of asymmetry, I understand intuition to be an intersubjective phenomenon: a two-way affair that, in addition to producing content that may be shared, aims at generating more capacious containers and better tools for thinking. I would therefore like to use the clinical case presented in the following section to demonstrate that intuition should not be understood just as a sudden comprehension or the illumination of a particular moment (perhaps experienced only by the analyst) but, rather, be seen as a process of analyst-patient co-construction that develops over time and that can lead to an understanding that is shared and emotionally sustainable. In developing this argument, I will begin by examining the relationship between the sensuous dimension and the psychic one in order then to pass to the relationship between memory, desire and hallucinosis and, subsequently, to the translatability and thinkability of an intuition.

The "sensuous" and the psychic dimensions

> The psycho-analyst and his analysand are alike dependent on the senses, but psychic qualities, with which psycho-analysis deals, are not perceived by the senses but, as Freud says, by some mental counterpart of the sense organs, a function that he attributed to consciousness.
>
> (Bion, 1970, p. 244)

Between the two dimensions that Bion distinguishes, moreover, there exists a constant dialectic relationship. On the one hand, there is the multisensory, concrete "sensuous" dimension, marked by an immediate hedonic tone and linked both to the pleasure/pain principle and to memory and desire; on the other, there is the psychic dimension that develops through the work of the alpha function, which transforms sensory elements to the point where "psychic qualities" are perceptible. The Grid's genetic axis offers a representation of this evolution that proceeds from the concrete to the abstract. As G. Civitarese writes, through a process of de-sensorialization /de-concretization/ abstraction, one passes from the β elements to the α elements, then to dream thoughts and so on. There is both a removing of differences between interdependent or contiguous terms (metonymy, in terms of rhetoric) and a transference between one element and another (metaphor). These processes of abstraction are reflected in the axis' downward development that serves for the formation of thought.

(Civitarese, 2012)

Bion reminds us that,

A formulation has the quality of an abstraction only insofar as it is divorced from the sensuous background inherent in and essential to memory and desire. The abstract statement must not stimulate memory and desire though memory and desire have contributed elements to its formulation.

(Bion, 1970, p. 248)

Thus, if objects of memory and desire serve to identify a constant conjunction, it then becomes necessary to discard their characteristics so that the statement representing the constant conjunction may remain unsaturated.

Bion outlines a multi-dimensional and formless Real underpinning all the Grid's categories; one that evolves and – if it comes into contact with the analyst's intuition – can "become" in at-one-ment. All this refers to transformations in O, which Bion carefully distinguishes from those in K.[1]

The reality of O is unreachable and variable, and our intuitions are continually forming and disintegrating. The journey from the concreteness of the sensuous reality to the abstraction of the psychic one is a constant coming and going between the two dimensions and, consequently, one must imagine the Grid as a model animated by continuous oscillations from the top down and vice versa (as well as between left and right, on the horizontal "Uses" axis).

Memory, desire and hallucinosis

I consider that the term 'hallucinosis' may also be applied to the mental state of the analyst when such state is very significantly characterized by processes traceable to memory and desire. Of the various problems deriving from memory and desire that Bion describes, the stereotyped and mechanical use of theoretical models seems important to me: it can induce in the analyst a sort of hallucinosis that can lead him/her to – literally – not see the patient.

R. Britton and J. Steiner write about the "Overvalued Idea" as a representation that crystallizes, creating certainties and an illusory coherence of facts and phenomena in a patient's material:

> A *"sudden precipitating intuition"* in the analyst may be the harbinger of insight; however, its arrival can also resemble the emergence of delusional certainty. The difference between a creative use of a selected fact and the crystallization of an overvalued idea may not be immediately evident. It would be arrogant of an analyst to suppose that he was immune to the unconscious processes that might lead to the emergence of an overvalued idea masquerading as an intuitive insight.
>
> (Britton and Steiner, 1994, p. 1071)

Both in the patient and in the analyst, a "model" can be hypostasized and turn into stereotyped assertions and accounts organized around chronologies, causal connections and univocal attributions of meaning. Memory and desire steer and saturate preconceptions in such a way as to make the encounter with the corresponding realization sterile. Amongst the dimensions underpinning the analyst's hallucinosis one can count social representations and cultural models that, as G. Bateson wrote, are so obvious and common as to be "unconscious": pride of place, here, goes to a misunderstood model of therapy that sees the patient's problems in terms of "deviation" from a "model" to be pursued through the patient's treatment and readjustment. The desire to "treat" paves the way to forms of collusive acting out that are, in some way, predictable and almost ritualized within the model. In bad cases, this may generate a dynamic of collusion between analyst and analysand that ends up confirming and stabilizing the therapist's hallucinosis. Patients can sense that the analyst has not rid him/herself of the memory and desire, however, and can have the sensation of being "possessed by and contained in" his/her mental state (Bion, 1970, p. 256). We could say that, in these bad cases, collusive processes defensively strive to prevent "the emergence of an unknown, incoherent, formless void and an associated sense of persecution by the elements of an evolving O" (Bion, 1970, pp. 264–265). And yet, as Bion reminds us, the analyst must pass through a persecutory and then a depressive phase before providing an interpretation. The depressive aspects flow, I think, from feeling alone, cut off and lacking in the (not yet permitted!) relief at being able to experience moments of at-one-ment with the patient, whilst the persecutory phase is the one of doubt, confusion and the loss of individual boundaries that results from engaging with alienating trans-personal dimensions.

As stated earlier, countless configurations are active during the course of a session and these are all underpinned by a drive towards the truth and/or oriented in the opposite direction, towards hiding and diverting the quest for meaning. Paraphrasing Bion, who cites Freud in a letter to Lou Andreas-Salome, one could say that it is necessary to direct "a beam of intense darkness" (Grotstein, 2007) so as to parenthesize or destroy self-evident senses in order to proceed in the analytic exploration and not be saturated (or bombarded) by a flood of sensory data and/ or prefabricated meanings.

Intuition and its translatability

Thomas Ogden recalls how the form of thought that Bion calls "intuition" is rooted in the unconscious mind and how the Unconscious is free to view an experience from multiple vertices simultaneously (Ogden, 2016). I consider that what unites the vertices and allows one to pass from one to the other is an abstract configuration that identifies a set of unvarying relations. A sort of common factor from which metaphorical and/or metonymical ties can stem, connecting several situations in a single, complex representation characterized by an opening up to new meanings.

The quest for meaning implies an unsaturated quality. It proceeds to an assimilation, on the one hand, and to the narcotization[2]/destruction of other senses or meanings,[3] on the other. As already stated, that results (both for the analyst and for the analysand) in loneliness, tension resulting from keeping explosive sensations and thoughts to oneself and a sense of loss regarding the destroyed thoughts. Maintaining an empty and unsaturated state of mind allows a transformative "space" to exist. Referring to what Julia Kristeva (1969) writes about modern poetry; it may be said that the configurations emerging during the intuitive process are not organized around "conjunctions" within a self-sufficient syntax that articulates its own meaning. Rather, they generate "alter-junctions", with the result that every element assimilates or opposes and negates other, simultaneously present configurations.

Intuition may bring one into contact with unusual and alienating dimensions, with objects and events placed in non-Euclidean spaces, with more than three dimensions and with objects immersed in non-linear (i.e. frozen, synchronous or reversible) temporalities: all multidimensional events that are not (yet) thinkable. Not by chance, Bion tells us that, through a suspension of memory, desire and understanding, the analyst has to "become infinite"! However, because of the impossibility of conceiving infinite dimensions, the object of the intuition must nevertheless be "three-dimensionalized" (Ginzburg, 2012) and – to differing degrees – made concrete in order to become representable.[4] In this respect, one may recall that Bion writes that thought is necessary when representing an intuition for private communication but also restrictive, as far as the transformation of preverbal material into alpha-elements is concerned. The ability to tolerate the frustration flowing from this restriction is fundamental for the establishing of a sense of reality and the development of thought.

The activity of representation requires an evolution of O and, at the same time, uses K-related functions and content in order to translate it. As a consequence, I see the transformations occurring during sessions as hinge-processes operating between the representable and the un-representable and generating a series of transitions not only from the sensory to the psychic but also in the opposite

direction. The fact that intuition is based on a work of abstraction that frees material from the factual aspect of sensory elements, from memory and from desire
does not imply that it must express a detached, disembodied psychic level that
is irreducibly in conflict with the sense dimension; it is, rather, fundamental that
the intuition is capable of summarizing and representing such dimension. In this
respect, the examples that most easily spring to mind are those involving artistic
creation, animated as this is by the dialectic tension between abstract and concrete. I believe that what Bion writes about the language of achievement may be
understood in this way.

The case of Luca

Luca is 39 years old and lost his mother at the age of 12. One day she had to go
to hospital; she told him that she would come back soon, after which he never
saw her or heard from her again. He learned of her death a couple of months
after her funeral service had taken place. His father (a doctor who had a drink
problem) gave him sketchy and muddled explanations, seeking refuge from the
matter in silence. He quickly found himself another companion and Luca sus-
pects that the relationship already existed while his mother was still alive. Luca
suffers from phobias: a flying phobia, in particular, but also one about enclosed
spaces such as lifts. It is as though it were "for ever" when they close the airplane hatch. He feels his experience of panic is like the one he had with his
mother during the time of her illness. He has never stopped tormenting himself
with the question as to why she did not at least phone him during the time she
was in hospital.

Right from the very first month of analysis, weekend breaks are accompanied by a
very marked malaise. So is the break caused by a mid-weekday when we do not see
each other. Luca feels abandoned and senses that he is detaching himself, "freezing
everything" and losing every memory of the relationship with me in his turn. His
mother's going away for a few days turned into a definitive disappearance. For him,
every leave-taking is "forever". The beginning of every new week is imbued with
conflicting emotions: resentment, the need to have a person beside him and fear that
such a strong need makes him dependent and despicable. With its tangle of explosive and therefore frozen emotions, the experience he lived with his mother seems
to remain physically at the centre of the room, untransformable: the experience of
absence repeats itself. D.W. Winnicott (1974) has written about how the "fear of
breakdown" is the fear of a breakdown that has already been experienced. Luca lost
his mother and did not have anyone who could hold him and help him "suffer" that
loss in the Bionian sense. He finds it impossible to put the loss of his mother in the
past because he continually expects to re-experience it. We could say, along with
Winnicott, that the traumatic event has happened but has not yet been experienced, in
the sense of being able to be shared and brought into current experience.

On the other hand, Luca cannot bear shame, feeling different or being pitied for
having been hit by such a disaster. He cannot bear being the inconsolable little orphan

who is so badly in need of love and understanding. This condition reduces him to an intolerable state of shame. He cannot manage to transform his hunger for relationship and warmth and his desire to be noticed and understood into something he can tolerate and this because his bond with me comes under violent attack. As a result, Luca's "desire" for us to re-find ourselves – like the one to re-find his mother inside himself – cannot translate into hope because it is too laden with the "grievance, regret, or remorse" referred to earlier and because it is too intense and desperate.

In his dreams but also and primarily (given that for a period he does not report any dreams) in the phantasies that he brings to sessions (telling me about films he has seen, for example), the figures of maltreated, abused children alternate with sadistic psychopaths and serial killers. I try to interpret these intensely ambivalent feelings, telling him that, in his relationship with me, he is living the experience of being abandoned – the same thing he felt with his mother – and that he is experiencing me as someone who stops thinking about him between sessions and deliberately neglects him without worrying about how dreadful he is feeling (the lack of interest that Luca experienced as a result of his father's inattentive attitude was also converging in the transference, I believe). I talk about how all of this provokes feelings of rage, despair and shame in him. I try to re-examine the "characters" that he has evoked, presenting them as expressions not only of the abusive behaviour to which he feels I am subjecting his inner child or his tender, childlike aspects, but also of his fear of hurting me as a result of his destructive rage. Despite the efforts I make when interpreting these feelings, Luca does not seem to draw any comfort from what I tell him.

After almost one year of analysis, the first summer break (greatly feared by him) arrives. *A posteriori*, I believe it was necessary for us to have to concretely, actually take our leave of each other for a longer period than usual in order, then, to be able to think it was possible to find each other again. After the summer, something seems to change for Luca. At work, they suggest he make some trips by train. He accepts and tells me he needs "freedom, fresh air". He is pleased about travelling with two nice, attractive female colleagues. He accepts without thinking about his diary and realizes afterwards that he will miss a day of therapy. He wants to go but is afraid he will have a panic attack, like he does in airplanes. Inside him, there is the child who feels "inadequate" and can be derided.

One day, while he is talking about "suffocating" relationships and telling me that he is afraid of becoming like Dr. Jekyll and Mr. Hyde, an outdoors scene suddenly and vividly presents itself before my eyes, interrupting the flow of my thoughts for an instant: a man on top of a massive wall is throwing a bottle down at me. Then I see the writing "SOS challenge" (in English) floating in the air. I try to understand something of that reverie's meaning. Someone is throwing bottles. Is it Mr. Hyde, the psychopath who represents an explosive reaction to suffocating, claustrophobic relationships based on the blackmail of abandonment? There is the desperate request for help and, at the same time, the challenge; not just the challenge of a duel with the other, I believe, but also the challenge with oneself, to prove that you are not afraid and are autonomous.

At the next session, he extols the virtues of his two colleagues and then says he wants to go, taking an anxiolytic with him. He has bought a book by a cognitive psychologist who explains techniques for controlling the fear of flying (the preface has been written by an Italian astronaut, U. Guidoni). I feel I've been put in the position of someone who is being left alone: after all, there are the colleagues and the book that he's taking (maybe not a "Guido", who makes you do analysis, but a "Guidoni",[5] who takes you into orbit with him?). At the same time, I tell myself it is important that Luca is able to have some fresh air and "deal" with his fears.

Stability and freedom seem to be irreconcilable during therapy. When I talk to him about this during a subsequent session, he tells me with a hint of indignation that he wants to "pick" at things in analysis; that analysis must help him to travel because, for him, it is only a "medical relationship". I can feel he is disappointed because analysis is not a painless journey. One day I tell him that it seems to me he is afraid of suffering a great deal if he continues with it. "Really?" he says to me. "That makes me laugh; I feel upset". His chest heaves with great sobs: "I'm laughing and crying". He talks about the fact that he does not know when the analysis will end. Perhaps he would like it to last forever but that scares him.

During the following session, he talks to me about survival: when the SOS is called, he must try to save himself all by himself because you cannot save yourself together with another person. When he feels abandoned, it is like being in the middle of the sea at night with the ship sailing away from you: "And then I think . . . we're dead!" After uttering this sentence, he is amazed that he has spoken in the plural instead of the singular: he should have said, "I'm dead". He thinks it was a slip of the tongue. I tell him that although he was living the disappearance of everything, for a split second he managed to think that people can be together and die together in that moment of togetherness. Something that was impossible when his mother died; when he felt that a part of himself was dying with her and he survived in the end but found he was alone. Perhaps now, however, we can begin to think that we can not only die but also survive together, him and I, and find ourselves again after the catastrophe.

We are at the end of the session and during the final minute we both maintain a silence that is charged with emotion. His dead mother and his "dead" himself can begin to find a space in which they may be recognized and differentiated: for one, there can be a "burial" and the possibility of a memory that is less violent and traumatic and, for the other, the first hint of a hope of life.

Concluding remarks

The case I have presented shows how an analyst's reverie can be linked to a patient's later, "intuitive" *lapsus linguae* and the analyst's subsequent intuition and conclusive interpretation. The reverie becomes part of an intuitive process shared by analyst and patient; a process that develops over time, following the thread of the invariants.

Antonino Ferro sees reverie as a highly specific phenomenon that offers the analyst's mind the possibility of coming into direct contact

> with one of the pictograms constituting the waking dream thought continually produced by the alpha function that constantly generates sequences of pictograms. That is to say, the possibility of coming into contact with a little bit of oneiric thought produced by the mind *in statu nascendi*.
>
> (Ferro, 2019, p. 589: our translation)

Reverie in this sense must, naturally, be distinguished from reverie understood as a maternal capacity or as a factor of the alpha function.

In an inter-subjective perspective and no differently from the intuition from which it must nevertheless be distinguished, reverie is the expression of a common area shared by patient and therapist. It is the result of a joint construction that gives voice to protoemotions in search of a representation. Naturally, it needs further working-through and cannot be communicated to the patient directly. As far as my own experience is concerned, the reverie I have described in this case involving Luca appeared in my mind with a sort of hyper-clarity that, for a second, dwarfed every thought and perception. It vividly placed the two positions alongside one another: request for help/SOS and "challenge". A challenge that was also expressed in the throwing of the bottle. Or might the bottle also contain an SOS, perhaps? The bottle certainly arrived like a missile.

The patient's challenge in seeking fresh air, the female colleagues (one of whom was to become his girlfriend), the book with the techniques for mastering the fear of flying and the astronaut Guidoni all constitute, on the one hand, a distancing from the analysis or form of contestation but, on the other, the possibility of developing the possibilities intrinsic to analysis: possibilities that may allow Luca a way out of the untransformable reality of losing his mother and the tangle of emotions accompanying it.

Through the invariant of the SOS, my reverie was taken up by the patient in his *lapsus linguae* and this *lapsus* defined and redirected the intuition process within a shared process. This made the analyst's intuition and subsequent interpretation possible, and these reunited the transferential events with those involving the maternal figure: "I am" or "We are"? Alone or with someone else? Alive or dead?

The closeness to the patient and the inter-subjective sharing made it possible to live, together, the moment of detachment both from the mother and from the analyst, as well as the condition of falling overboard into a night sea. They made it possible to live, together, the death, the extinguishing of every hope and the severance of every tie. They made it possible to live, together, the passage from life to death and from death to life. Thus, they created a first possibility of living the grief linked to the loss of Luca's mother and surviving the emotional tsunami together (tsunamis were often present in his dreams), so as to then be able to open up to life.

Notes

1 I would argue that achieving contact with psychic reality, namely, the evolved characteristics of the O domain, suggests having a "vision" rather than knowing; a conjectural or abductive thinking rather than a hypothetical-deductive one. It is a thinking that takes account of clues, signs and unconscious perceptions linking different phenomena, a thinking that grasps a reality before being able to explain how or why, in order to bring it to the analysand's attention, where appropriate. The Italian philosopher R. Fabbrichesi (2018) has written about conjectural thought (as distinct from hypothetical-deductive thought) from the classical Greek philosophical tradition to C. Peirce's reflections on abduction. She analyses the meaning of Greek terms such as the verb *tekmairesthai*: "the act of conjecturing, via signs and clues, the correct course to follow, the choosing of points of reference so as to throw down a gangway between the visible and the invisible". Bion writes in "*Attention and Interpretation*" that the analyst must have a "capacity for conjecture".
2 U. Eco (1979) has written about parts of a text that are "magnified" and stressed and about others that are neglected or "narcotized".
3 Here I am referring to the distinction Bion draws between "sense" and "meaning".
4 Following I. Matte Blanco's thinking, the author writes, for example, of how the unconscious can render the idea of the infinite by representing it, in dreams, through a huge number of individuals or a single example possessing a characteristic in the highest degree.
5 In Italian, the suffix – *one* (singular) or – *oni* (plural) has an augmentative function. Thus the astronaut's name, "Guidoni" could be taken to mean "big Guido(s)"; a fact open to interpretation.

References

Bion, Wilfred R. (1967a). Second Thoughts. Selected Papers on Psychoanalysis. In C. Mawson (Ed.), *The Complete Works of W.R. Bion*. Vol. VI. London: Karnac Books, 2014.

Bion, Wilfred R. (1967b). Notes on Memory and Desire. In C. Mawson (Ed.), *The Complete Works of W.R. Bion*. Vol. VI. London: Karnac Books, 2014.

Bion, Wilfred R. (1970). Attention and Interpretation. In C. Mawson (Ed.), *The Complete Works of W.R. Bion*. Vol. VI. London: Karnac Books, 2014.

Britton, R., and Steiner, R. (1994). Interpretation: Selected Fact or Overvalued Idea? *International Journal of Psychology*, 75: 1069–1078.

Civitarese, G. (2012). La griglia e la pulsione di verità. *Rivista Di Psicoanalisi*, 58(2): 335–360. Eng. Trans. The Grid and the Truth Drive. *The Italian Psychoanalytic Annual*, 2013, 7: 91–114.

Eco, Umberto. (1979). *Lector in Fabula*. Milan: Bompiani.

Fabbrichesi, R. (2018). Segno e congettura. Breve storia dell'abduzione. *Psiche: Rivista Di Cultura Psicoanalitica*, 2: 379–395.

Ferro, A. (2019). Reverie. *Rivista Di Psicoanalisi*, 65(3): 589–593.

Ginzburg, A. (2012). Il sogno e la rivelazione di verità dissociate. *Rivista Di Psicoanalisi*, 58(2): 419–434.

Grotstein, James S. (2007). *A Beam of Intense Darkness*. London: Karnac Books.

Kristeva, Julia. (1969). *Sèméiotikè. Recherches pour une sémanalyse*. Paris: Éditions du Seuil.

Ogden, Thomas H. (2016). *Reclaiming Unlived Life*. London: Routledge.

Winnicott, Donald W. (1974). Fear of Breakdown. *The International Review of Psycho-Analysis*, 1: 103–107.

Chapter 5

Intuition

Privileged tool to access the primordial mind

Alicia Beatriz Dorado de Lisondo, Naly Durand, and Mariângela Mendes de Almeida

Introduction

Intuition is a valuable form of knowledge. Its etymology derives from the Latin *intuitĭo, ōnis* "image reflected in the mirror." Also, from the Latin arises *intuire*, which means to consider, see inside, or contemplate. The intuitive mind opens to the new, creative, and unknown.

Always a direct apprehension, intuition is an immediate and complete knowledge (Alves, 2019) that is not taught or induced. As Viera de Camargo (2019) points out, it is a pre-reflective capture of an immediate reality.

For the analyst in a state of faith, intuition is the privileged way to reach the O, the ultimate reality, unknowledgeable in its essence.

Intuition in Bion

In *Elements of Psychoanalysis*, Bion (1963) recommends using the grid to approach the analyst-patient's flows within the session. Considering the category of dream thoughts, dreams, and myths, an "operating intuition, a minimum degree of intuitive capacity and intuitive health" may be exercised as part of the psychoanalytic domain as our psychoanalytic personality develops within our analysis, re-analysis, and emotional experience with our patients (Bion, 1992).

Bion's technical recommendation regarding the suspension of predefined memory, desire, understanding and apprehension of the senses will be a huge ally to better observe and elaborate imaginative conjectures as attempts to approach the primordial mind.

To conquer certain freedom concerning memory, desire, and understanding, which in *Cogitations* (1992) Bion considers "opacities which obstruct intuition," discipline needs to be permanent, lasting, and continuous. The psychoanalytic flow is not facilitated by the obstructive memory that uses the past as refuge, possession and thus saturates the field with what is already known as conscious memories and pre-existing knowledge. This memory quality is not favourable to

DOI: 10.4324/9781003293385-6

allow dream-like memories that arise from the analyst's (or patient's) alpha dream work during the session.

The determinism of the positive sciences amputates the contributions of quantum physics to scientific epistemology. Arising from the drives and launching into the future, the pre-determined desire saturates the possibilities of discovery, obstructing the K link within the analyst's mind. Desire and memory are two sides of the same coin. Both saturate the mind with sensory elements. Desire is different from the expectation, faith, and hope mentioned by Bion.

For the analyst, pursuing the fulfilment of his own wishes or the patient's family's wishes obstructs psychic contact. *Furor curandis* may then prevail.

Allowing the uncertain and the unknown requests excluding the active "desire to understand" and the need to fit the experience into a theoretical reference.

The "memory of what is already understood" needs to be abandoned, opening space to an indeterminate time instead of the usual categories of space, time, and causality. This patiently tolerated state will avoid the "irritating search for facts and reasons" but may expose the analyst to the frustration of not understanding.

Bion's contributions exceed the Freudian indication of "floating attention" by inviting a state of flotation of virtually all ego functions, a "floating mind," which temporarily suspends the notation, attention, judgment, and importance attributed to the sense organs (Bianchedi, 2016).

Observation in Bion

The analyst must have his mind as analysed as possible to contain the emotional impact of the experience, allowing the emergence of the new. This discipline requires containment, negative capability, tolerance for the sense of infinity, frustration, patience, and renunciation of prejudices.

Within this attitude, tolerance for the unknown is paired with confidence that "something" will evolve in the emotional contact with the patient and that "something" can be observed.

For intuition to be recognized as a way of accessing knowledge, the negative capability needs to come into play. The poet Keats defined it as the condition for accepting uncertainty as something beautiful and humanized. Just as Freud follows the lessons of Charcot, when he wrote that he needed to blind himself artificially to concentrate the weakest flash of light on a very dark situation, Bion (1977a, pp. 28–29) transforms this analogy to consider the importance of "artificial silence" when it is necessary to hear "very weak noises." Darkening to see is analogous to deafening to hear. For Dario Sor (2014/2016, p. 39), you can achieve "a kind of sensory alternation, opaque one sense to stimulate another, do not hear in order to see, do not see in order to hear." This increases infrasensorial and suprasensorial perception. The analyst who has come into contact with his primordial mind in his personal analysis and his clinical experience will have psychic growth and increase his intuitive capacity.

Intuition and knowledge

Braga (2019) emphasizes that Bion (1992), by giving a crucial place to intuition, freed psychoanalysis of the chains of the nineteenth-century science mechanistic view. For them, observation and intuition form a constantly conjugated pair.

Intuition is the immediate direct vision and understanding of a truth. This knowledge is sometimes confused with a mystical vertex.

Intuition allows us to be surprised by the evolving of the patient's unconscious, being then a privileged tool in the analytic process.

In *Attention and Interpretation*, Bion (1970) considers intuition as a mental equivalent to sense organs.

Intuition earns its citizenship card in the context of discovering a science in correlation with the observed, the eureka when the new idea emerges. This form of knowledge opposes rational, traditional scientific knowledge.

That sensory impression is represented in the psyche as a visual image, an ideogram, and many times as incipient possible registers of turmoil and turbulence, proto or pre-stages in the intuitive field. Could these be associated with embrionary stages within the routes to contact with this kind of knowledge?

The primordial mind and possible links with intuition

Bion (1977a/1982, p. 54), in his work on caesura, writes:

> The embryologist speaks about "optic pits" and "auditory pits." . . . Is there any part of the human mind that still betrays signs of an "embryological" intuition, either visual or auditory? . . . there is a connection between postnatal thinking and emotional life and prenatal life. Using exaggeration to simplify: Should we consider that the foetus thinks, feels, sees, or hears?

Bion (1976a), in his scientific fictions, points out that the relationship between germplasm and the environment operates from an incredibly early stage. He says that even after the impressive caesura of birth (Bion, 1977a), this relationship can leave marks.

Certain states of intense fear can be seen if we consider them a thalamic fear or a type of glandular manifestation of the renal-related type.

One could conjecture that under certain variations in the amniotic fluid pressure, the foetus could see an intolerable bright light and hear intolerable loud sounds. The remains of a very primitive sensitivity could continue throughout life.

In *Evidence* Bion (1976b, pp. 245, 246) says:

> I imagine a situation in which a foetus almost at birth would detect extremely unpleasant oscillations in the environment provided by the amniotic fluid before passing into a gaseous environment, in other words, before birth. I

imagine there are some disturbances, parents without a good relationship, or something like that. I can also imagine that the father and mother make loud noises, . . . Suppose this foetus also detects what will one day become the character or personality, detects things like fear, hate, such basic emotions.

Then, the omnipotent foetus, at an incredibly early stage, could become hostile to these disturbing feelings, proto-ideas, proto-feelings, divide them, destroy them, fragment them and try to evacuate them.

(Bion, 1976b, pp. 245, 246)

Freud (1926) reformulates the theory of anguish and addresses the trauma of birth, bringing up the idea of caesura.

CarlosTabbia (2018, p. 4) reminds us that "the fertilized egg creates the placenta to be held." This semipermeable membrane, linking and separating, is a large surface for the exchange of different materials through the placental membrane. We conjecture that it is also through the placenta that the circulation of sensations and protoemotions occurs.

Susan Maiello (2012) shows in clinical work that the uterine container is not only a physical reality but that this reality can be connected to original prenatal protomental experiences.

We inquire, hoping that our clinical vignettes that follow (each one of a patient seen by one of the authors) will illustrate and motivate possible conjectures:

- Could it be that these prenatal sensations do not always reach the possibility of symbolic expression in verbal, preverbal, artistic language, and may then be compulsively repeated?
- And is it not the intuition that feeds the imaginative conjectures, the analyst's alpha dream work, the ideograms that inspire interpretation?
- Would tolerance of chaos and turbulence of a very primitive quality, like what we experience since our primordial times, contribute to allow, and enrich "intuitive capacity and intuitive health"?

(Bion, 1992)

Clinical material

Thiago: a picture in mind

An adolescent adopted at 6 months of age; Thiago began his analysis with me when he was 15 years old. He had also been treated as a child.

Anthropologists studying a Xingu tribe in Brazil found him and hid him because his mother had died during childbirth and his father had abandoned him. According to the cultural tradition in the tribe, his destiny would have been to be sacrificed in a community ritual for considered guilty of his mother's death. He was seen as a transgressor of the Divine Order.

Away from the tribe, this baby had several milkmaids and was taken from village to village until a couple, already parents of a child, accepted him for adoption. The adopted parents had had a positive experience with their first son, which inspired them to adopt Thiago. When Thiago arrived, the mother was pregnant with another baby.

Thiago arrived malnourished, rickety, with malaria, diarrheas, breathing difficulties, and shaved hair and eyebrows. He needed to have several blood transfusions.

Thiago cried all the time and swallowed the milk which ran into his throat without using his lips to suck; he bit everything around him. "He looked like he had come from a concentration camp. He was skin and bones," the parents said.

He had a somatic vulnerability, with diarrhea being constant up to 3 years of age. He feared physical contact, isolated himself from family life with hostility and presented great difficulties in schooling.

As an adolescent, Thiago was described to me as a strange, difficult, solitary creature without any occupation in life. When his father tried to talk to him while seated next to him in a car, Thiago turned his head 45 degrees to create distance. What will the future of his son be? This was the reason for the consultation for these parents, whose intellectual interests seemed to contrast with how the adolescent presented himself to them. However, to me and in his analysis, we were introduced to an essential interest and truthful search for primitive knowledge of his own self and life.

I began the treatment with four weekly sessions. Thiago made good use of his space. He always arrived late to the sessions. He entered rapidly, placing the box in front of himself, almost touching his body. In the very tight space remaining on the table, he would draw. He always came heavily dressed, with skate boots. He used to bring a skateboard and/or a backpack hanging in front of his chest. I think that in this way, he made up for the lack of an exoskeleton with a reinforced breastplate, a second skin (Bick, 1968).

Five minutes before his hour was up, when the alarm of his watch sounded, he would ask: *When do I come back?* Or *How much time have we been together?*

He frequently missed the sessions without giving any notice. I used to call him by phone within his session time to acknowledge that I was waiting for him, trying to create a link, make myself present, show my interest and place him in contact with reality in time and space.

On his arrival to our room, he usually ran to the chair to sit facing the table and not next to me; he drew brilliantly, using his box as a wall to avoid eye contact and to hide from me. Sometimes he used to look at me as if he were spying on me. When he finished drawing, he used to throw the drawing onto the box.

Interestingly, with the box between us, I felt curious and protected. The box, countertransferentially, might have been felt like a protective wall for me. The primitive power of life and death involved in the images he produced might have been too powerful.

In the session, when he drew the picture shown here, he placed the drawing onto his box and crouched down. Like in the drawing, it was as if he was getting smaller, as he put himself in a foetal position. I thought, without interpreting, that the box between us was the denial of the link, but at the same time, the very existence of the link. I experienced this box like a paradox, a caesura.

Within the analytic space, he repeated what he used to do with the analytic time. He denied that the session had a beginning and an end; in that way, there was almost neither encounter nor separation. There was no death, no history, no frustration. There was only a programmed mechanical noise that indicated a sharp hour, a chronology of events. In his secret, magic, and tyrannic omnipotence, he turned the analytic scene into a circular space and time without beginning nor end, just like a bidimensional area.

On the other hand, we witnessed the emergence of fascinating drawings of atavistic leftovers, a savage past-present, sensorial evacuations mixed up with shapes from another level of psychic structure, capsulized remains preserved in singular images (Tustin, 1934; Rosenfeld, 1991), animistic thoughts alive on the paper (Freud, 1912). We could see the artist enslaved by the secret magic. In the images, his ideograms with bizarre objects were delineated: faces, sharp shapes, a dragon, monsters.

I observed the drawing as if it was a piece of artwork.

The drawings and their further shared exploration guaranteed the presence of an inner world, even if eccentric. Brought to our transferential field, nothing ran the risk of being lost. This was his possibility of existing, of finding a language within his analytical process. I want to emphasize that in the drawing, among the strange ancestral, scary, and enigmatic figures that evoked a pre-historical world to me, a fetus appeared and was highlighted by me. It came to my mind intuitively that the baby in the picture, before being born, connected us to the presence of a primordial mind and prenatal life. The sensorial registers had left marks in the unconscious, but they had remained without a name. With that fetus in my soul and in my mind, I was encouraged to think of his potential capacities that had not been born yet.

Thiago showed me his dark astonished and mysterious inner world.

I interpreted, "Here between the terrible monsters, there are also pretty shapes which I have met" and I showed him in the drawing.

Later in the same session, I said: "But here (right side of the paper), there are also two human figures struggling to find ground to stand on. Thiago, as the fetus, wants to take care of the analysis, to be born as a human being, to grow." I showed the figures to him.

The development of the transferential and counter-transferential relationship allowed the life and death dilemma to return in Thiago's "psychic rebirth' within the analytical process. Thiago wanted to know if I really accepted him at a gut level being the way he was, if he would be 'adopted' as a patient by me, without me risking my own life as an analytic mind, allowing for his birth. Could we be a

Figure 5.1 Fetus drawing

surviving mother-infant dyad in a successful psychic labour, a surviving analytic couple?

When I found a fetus in his drawing amid lots of ancestral, terrifying, and threatening figures (see Figure 5.1), intuitive channels connected me with the scenario of his prenatal and postnatal life. Those dreadful figures, which could be associated with transgenerational mandates with the mission to interrupt life, might have permeated his birth with the risk of death and evoked in me the agony and turmoil which his primordial life might have been filled with. This state of permeability to the unknown and chaos in me and the patient might have preceded the possibility for us to intuitively approach and connect with his prenatal and postnatal unborn experience.

How could we talk about self and others with someone conceived in such a complex and dark web of affect relationships?

What was the crib woven for Thiago in the imaginary world of his parents? What was the ambush where Oedipus was conceived?

As a fetus-self with a round and tender human face, wouldn't Thiago be begging for his primordial mind to be seen, welcome, and understood? And wouldn't this be a way of claiming for psychic survival?

Eugenia: the pool of terror

The parents of Eugenia, a 4-year-old girl, bring her to me because she does not speak in the presence of strangers. She is an only daughter and only expresses herself verbally with them, but with other relatives, in the nursery, or when she is left in the nanny's care, she falls into her habitual silence.

The pregnancy of Eugenia's mother was initially of twins. At the fourth month of pregnancy, the male twin's growth stopped, for which they had to do a curettage, extracting the amniotic sac with the intrauterine baby. This issue was kept silent by the parents, among themselves and with the girl. For them, Eugenia "did not know" of the existence of that little brother.

There were no difficulties in labour, neither in the rest of the girl's development, except for her selective mutism after having learned to speak without difficulties for about a year and a half, according to the parents.

The beginning of this treatment was marked by silence. She had no difficulty entering and staying alone with me. After a few hours of family play, she looked at me with her big, astonished eyes and smiled at me but did not speak. She played a repetitive game for months, in which she took all the dolls, babies and animals out of their box, placed them sitting in a row on the couch and made them interact, moving them, in silence.

The game evolved and each time, she allowed me to participate more. We fed the dolls, put them to bed and made them sleep. She persisted in her silence, and I sometimes spoke, as in storytelling, what we were doing, including interpretations. She was looking at me and as time went by, she began to answer me with monosyllables.

In one of the sessions, she changes that repetitive game, empties her box, and places all the babies inside. She looks at me while she opens, rounding her mouth as if she is screaming. A silent scream of terror seems to come out.

Shocked by the scene, I tell her that something scares the babies a lot, that they seem as if they want to scream and cannot.

She looks at me and says, "It's the pool of terror," putting together a complete sentence for the first time.

"What makes you so terrified?" I ask, taking advantage of the beginning of a dialogue and using the word terror that she had used.

"The bad guys are coming to kill them," she answers.

"Let us save them! Can we do something?" I offer.

"No," she answers categorically.

"And if we try?" I insist, extending my hands towards the pool of terror.

She pushes them away from the "pool of terror," quickly takes two or three babies and throws them on the ground, saying, "There it is."

Impressed by the clarity of the language and the representation of what I intuited was a sensory impression that could have been registered in the psyche during her intrauterine state, I ask, "What is it there?" "It is gone!" she answers me curtly.

She returns to her usual silence, refusing to continue talking about that game in that session. But the game, with an intense emotional connotation, was repeated for a long time. Sometimes she allowed me to save a baby and other times, she did not.

I found myself surprised by what it seemed to me an ability to express symbolically in verbal and playful language, protomental experiences, prenatal and pre-verbal sensations. And by not putting words about the missing brother, the parents prevented her from communicating language with the people around her, except with themselves. Eugenia shared this never revealed secret with them, which I have the intuition that the little girl unconsciously already knew. Intuition emerges here as an experience both for the patient and for the analyst, thus shared within the analytic relationship and perhaps allowed by the tolerance to chaos, death, and terror within the analyst's uterine mind in contact with protomental states.

Supported by the girl's game's evolution, I was encouraged to interpret her intrauterine terrors and the dialogue became more fluid and the games diversified.

After a while, Eugenia, now a girl of more than 5 years, tells me that she is playing at being a doctor during a session, that she wants to be a baby doctor. I ask her if she wants to heal the babies and she says no, she wants to help the mothers so that their babies may be born well.

Of course, this little girl surprises me again with her intuition, which I would be encouraged to conjecture as "quasi-reparatory," which I consider going beyond known theories and for which I have no answer.

Based on what Eugenia shows us, the questions exceed the experiences that an intrauterine baby can mean after birth. Considering what was lived in our primordial mind, can we think of reparative attempts based on certain primitive knowledge acquired along with pregnancy? Or is it just a proto mental intuition, with no memory, no desire, no understanding?

Outside the session, I returned to the last Bion and his scientific fictions (1977b) when he points out that the relationship between germplasm and the environment operates from an incredibly early stage and that this relationship can leave marks. He further conjectures that certain states of terror originate from the thalamus and its unmyelinated nerve connections, and that the remnants of a very primitive sensitivity could continue throughout life. Meltzer (1988) also accompanied me in my theoretical explorations, with his imaginative conjectures of the intrauterine baby and Carlos Tabbia (2018) as well, when he speaks that, through the placenta, the circulation of sensations and affect can take place.

Pablo: surviving turmoil together

In the following vignette, the house where the analyst's consulting room has been located used to be the past analyst's family house. Very recently, the children's practice has moved to the room that used to be originally the children's bedroom, somehow an "archaic familiar place," in which, however, a completely new experience starts every session with each patient. It was not different with Pablo, a pre-adolescent boy who has been in analytical process for nine years, having suffered from intense inner states of anxiety and contact difficulties of autistic quality, with an extreme need to control his feeding choices and routines.

In a session when we were sharing his incipient opening to spontaneous social links, we were both astonished with many papers falling from a cabinet near the ceiling, after a sudden opening in front of us, just above the entrance to the room.

To our surprise, while I was internally dealing with that impact (considering in a condensed turmoil flash also my own personal associations to be described soon), he was the first to speak, a bit frightened. With a light sense of humor that put into words the shock I was also experiencing, he said: "We are in Japan!!!"

I had heard from a previous patient that day that there was a secret passage through the same little door of that cabinet and that I used to live there! With that patient, we had talked about an inner place where we live with our thoughts, dreams, an inner place that is secret, but which brings us to our talks here.

It was unavoidable to bring back that experience when, later with Pablo, the high cabinet door at the top suddenly opened. I was shaken with the power of the surrounding intuitive material (from the previous patient and its possible triggering effect on me and my associative underlying level of nonverbal exchange in the analytic encounter with Pablo, also powerful in touching primitive developments in our analytic history). The "memory" that emerged then was not of a pre-existent, obstructive quality. Still, it was "brought into consciousness" (Bion, 1977), awakened by emotional experience, gathering impressions and expressions of primitive content in that psychic space where infantile aspects may inhabit and circulate.

"We are in Japan!!!" That metaphor expressed so vividly and promptly by Pablo seemed to figure out our world moving upside down as in an earthquake. It conveyed the sense of a psychic relationship that allowed him to represent a threat, in an expression to be heard and accompanied. It seemed to contain our "pieces," gathering irrational and archaic levels of experience with a symbolic capacity to face it.

Are we talking here about the need to be in a close link with protopsychic layers of both of us, patient and analyst, in the analytic encounter? At the same time, would there be a threat of being overwhelmed by primitive content to be processed? Without overloading the patient, helped by our own spaces for processing, we can share a quality of psychic depth to be explored within each singular context.

In Pablo's s case, this opening to social contact was actually an earthquake, with him getting more involved in talking and responding to friends on his cell phone and finding it particularly important to show me this new opening, which was there for us to share and witness in celebration.

At the same time in this very session, he had just talked by voice message to a friend who was inviting him to buy them tickets to go together to a theatre play and, in an impulsive familiar straight and cold response, he said he did not need that, because, as Pablo's father is a professional in the field, he could ask him at any time to go to that play (alone . . . or at the most with his family, dismissing that longed for peer invitation, that might have evoked an intense emotionality).

Hearing that "cut" breaking up links and contact, I felt myself as almost jumping from the chair and moving from a celebrating state of mind that seemed to be wished by him too, to a quick and sudden feeling of being shattered and swept away from any emotional appeal and attunement, of great autistic quality.

I could not avoid showing that surprise to him in my tone of voice and even subtle, bodily and facial reactions when I tried to understand with him why he had had to freeze that . . . I had to harbor in me, for him, the conflicting anxiety he was not yet able to experience . . . it was at that moment that we had the opening of that cabinet door!!!!

It was then that we "went to Japan" and that we were taken by who knows what kind of primitive witnessing of physical reality to make sense of its psychic content together.

In what kind of functioning, possibly involving physical, proto psychic and psychic elements within the same circuit (perhaps intuitive and infrasensorial movements in Bion's words), were we involved?

Near the end of the session, we had to deal with the concrete result of the papers fallen from the high cabinet above the door to go out of the room, opening our way and making sure that we could go through the door safely. While I was picking up a stairway just to make sure that there was not anything to fall on our heads when passing through, Pablo went to a big cushion in the room and calmly responded to his friend that yes, in second thoughts, he would like to go to the play with him, and when was he thinking of doing that?

Could those movements allowing new openings by Pablo and of us "going through the door" following the "catastrophe" be associated with experiencing the caesura, as dramatic transitions and changes from one state of mind to the other, allowing separations and mobility between points of junctures, links, synapses, thus giving birth to new experiences (Bion, 1977a)?

The analytic challenge to be sensitive to the impact within ourselves, with each's own singularities, allowed us to experience that fright together with emotional attunement. Could we envisage these "naked moments" in a raw state, before arriving at consciousness and definitions, as producing a built-together sense of attunement that is not explained rationally but which is felt like a true encounter between our minds?

How much was the analyst's link with one's own inner self, as touched by intuition and by the emotional experience in the session, essential for the patient to enlarge his own capacity to allow contact with the unexpected?

Final considerations

As we intended to show here, connecting theory and clinical vignettes, our capacity and training to be able to sustain the inner earthquake and upside-down turmoil in our own and our patients' primitive experiences, seems to be an expressive and fruitful field for intuition and perhaps a precondition for it to emerge.

Mainly through clinical approach, our Via Regia of investigation and intervention in psychoanalysis, we hope to have touched different levels of mental states, both in our patients and within ourselves. As psychoanalysts, we have the privilege and opportunity to access primitive, intuitive, and embrionary areas, which, as Bion says, may be buried in the future that has not happened or in the past that is forgotten and that can hardly be said to belong to what we call "thought" (Bion, 1977b).

We would like to thank Alberto Pieczansky for his English review of the text.

References

Alves, D. (2019). *Observar, perceber, intuir, conhecer – vida: Ideias em trânsito*. XII Jornada de Bion: SBPSP.

Bianchedi, E.T. (2016). Cambio Psíquico: El Devenir de una Indagación, Mentalización. In *Revista de psicoanálisis y psicoterapia*. Vol. 1. AIEDEM.

Bick, E. (1968). The Experience of the Skin in Early Object – Relation. *The International Journal of Psychoanalysis*, 49(2–3): 484–486.

Bion, W.R. (1963). *Elements of Psycho-analysis*. London: Heinemann Medical Books.

Bion, W.R. (1970). *Attention and Interpretation*. London: Tavistock Publications.

Bion, W.R. (1976a). On a Quotation from Freud. In W.R. Bion (Ed.), *Clinical Seminars and Four Papers*. UK: Radavian Press, pp. 234–238.

Bion, W.R. (1976b). Evidence. In W.R. Bion (Ed.), *Clinical Seminars and Four Papers*. UK: Radavian Press, pp. 239–248.

Bion, W.R. (1977a). *Two Papers: The Grid and Caesura*. Rio de Janeiro: Imago.

Bion, W.R. (1977b). *A Memoir of the Future*. Rio de Janeiro: Imago.

Bion, W.R. (1992). *Cogitations*. Ed. F. Bion. London: Karnac.

Braga, J.C. (2019). *¿Intuir é vislumbrar o inconsciente? Esmiuçando e posicionando algumas questões presentes na obra de Bion*. XII Jornada de Bion: SBPSP.

Camargo, C.A.V. (2019). *Observação e Intuição*. XII Jornada de Bion: SBPSP.

Freud, S. (1926). *Inhibición, síntoma y angustia*. Amorrortu: Buenos Aires. *S.E.* Vol. XX.

Maiello, S. (2012, December). Prenatal Experiences of Containment in the Light of Bion's Model of Container/Contained. *Journal of Child Psychotherapy*, 38(3): 250–267 (ISSN 0075-417X print/ISSN 1469-9370 online).

Rosenfeld, D. (1984). Hypochondrias, Somatic Delusion and Psychoanalytic Practice. *The International Journal of Psychoanalysis*, 65: 377–387.

Rosenfeld, D., and Lisondo Dorado, A. (1991). Un enfant qui cherche un enfant. *Journal de la Psychanalyse de L'enfant*. Trauma fascicule, no 9.

Rosenfeld, D., and Lisondo Dorado, A. *Drama and Hope in Adoption: 23 in Transference, Light on the Dilema*.

Sor, D. (2014/2016). Introducción y psicoanálisis. In *Psicoanálisis: Revista de la Asociación Psicoanalítica Colombiana*. Vol. XXVII, n° 2. Bogotá, CO, 2015.

Tabbia, C. (2018). *Modelo placentario de la intimidad*. Presented in Sevilla, Espanha.

Vallejo, A. (1985). *Vocabulário Lacaniano*. Argentina: Helgnero Editores.

Chapter 6

Intuitive comprehension and dreaming in child analysis

Teresa Rocha Leite Haudenschild

> Wanderer there is no path, the path you make as you walk.
> When walking the path is made, and when you look back
> you see the way that will never be walked again.
>
> (Machado, 1912)[1]

Introduction

In the analysis of children communication takes place through dramatization, play, drawings and narrations, understood as derived from the daytime oneiric thought of the analysand to be "re-dreamed" together with the analyst based on his availability and openness for listening. To be able to "re-dream", to reorganize the emotional elements staged in the session, the analyst must have a sufficient oneiric repertoire of emotional experiences already metabolized, as well as a sufficient repertoire of psychoanalytical theories evoked by the analysand's material,[2] since, as Kant states: "an intuition without a concept is blind; a concept without intuition is empty" (1787).

The analyst, by using his alpha function in a state of *reverie*, operates as an empathetic container for the protosensorial and protomental states of the analysand, in *unison* with the nature of their pain and emotions, "being with" and "dreaming" them (transformations in O). He may then propose some knowledge (transformation in K), and, based on the analysand's responses, modulate the analytical dialogue towards psychic growth.

Construction and amplification of psychic containment and transformations in dreams in the analysis of children

When Bion conceives of "transformations in dreams" he proposes that subjects see themselves in human relational situations, bringing continuity to Klein's intuition when she proposed communication with children through scenes constructed with small toys in which they could see themselves as if in a scene from a film. *Phantasein* in Greek means "to make visible". Through play, the child's place in

DOI: 10.4324/9781003293385-7

the human world becomes visible to them, just as their emotions are awakened in intersubjective relationships.

It is in this relational context that the subject can situate himself, find his place in the world, perceive himself and feel who he is. This *feeling of situation* (Heidegger, 1927) is the first step towards realizing his singular existence. The negation of this insertion (through autistic withdrawal, for example), or non-access to the human world, as in children with a deficit in early emotional development, leads them to being like entities subsisting within the world and, beyond this, within themselves, *worldless*: if they do not *touch each other emotionally*, they cannot be *close to the other* (Heidegger, 1927).

This *letting oneself be touched* by the existence of another human being, *being emotionally open* to the other, leads to *intuitive comprehension* and the attempt to communicate through meaningful "speech"[3] (Heidegger, 1954). Man is the only existent being, the only one who can give meaning to his life and to subsistent entities (plants, animals and inanimate objects). It is therefore "ek-sistence" – man's exposure to the world – that makes him a human being open to the unpredictable encounter with the world, with others, "there", "now", in which his own unknown possibilities can arise, and those of others, in co-existence (Heidegger, 1927).

Since human beings, in their facticity, cannot always live in "openness", at times the "speech" is "veiled", at others "unveiled".

For Merleau Ponty (1969) this "speech" is expressed through narration, theatrical plays, and visual and plastic arts. Such speech expresses subjectivity and for Bion is derived from oneiric thought.

In analytical sessions it is from the co-existence of contributions from the analysand and analyst that dreaming and thinking are co-generated as new fruits of each encounter.

Child analysis today

The objective of analytical treatment is to amplify contact with internal and external reality and reconstruct (or construct) the history of a singular existence, opening it up to a creative future based on the present of each session.

To do so, it is fundamental that there be an evaluation of the conditions of the psychical apparatus of the analysand for "thinking" reality, which Bion names the *alpha function*, that allows the transformation of protosensorial and protoemotional elements (*beta elements*) into psychic representations with emotional meanings. "Beta elements move psychic life. If they are not transformed, this life loses potentiality" (Ferro, 2007).

Some analysands arrive with a psychic apparatus already capable of thinking and "dreaming" reality, both by day (daytime oneiric thought) and at night (nocturnal dreaming thought). There are analysands who need to amplify this function and others who do not possess it yet and will have to begin to build it, as described in the clinical vignettes at the end of this paper.

The analyst, through their *reverie*, functions as a *comprehensive object* (Bion, 1962), disposed to receive, harbour, metabolize, name and explore meanings of the protosensorial and protoemotional contents communicated by analysands through their projective identifications. It is in this way that their capacity for contact with psychic reality and containment for their emotions grows.

When this capacity has not yet been constructed, the analyst must lend their *reverie* so that the analysand can, little by little, introject until they become sufficiently *self-containing* (Meltzer, 1975) of the elements of their psychic reality.

The introjection of containment is more important than the introjection of the internal representation of emotional contents, although both occur concomitantly. It is based on this introjection that the subject has a notion that they have an inner psychical space, an internal world, just as the object has, and these are unique.

Evaluation

To evaluate the predominant mental functioning and therefore the conditions of the analysand for contact with reality, it would be useful to think about a range of the functioning of mental states (see Figure 6.1).

Non-integrated states (studied by the post-Kleinians: Bick, Meltzer, Tustin, Alvarez, Haag, Athanassiou, Mitrani):

Anxieties are catastrophic in a world felt as one-dimensional where there are identifications with sensory points of sound, light, touch, smell, taste, or in

Mental Functioning

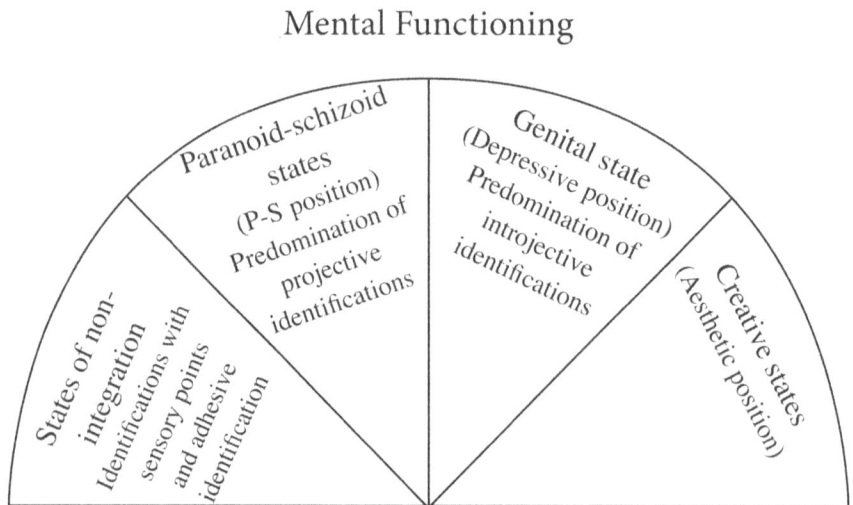

Figure 6.1 Mental functioning

a two-dimensional world of adhesive identifications with surfaces of sensory objects (sensation objects – Tustin, 1981; Mitrani, 2001).

In the one-dimensional world, *time* is equivalent to the distance from the object to be reached, in a movement of tropism. In the two-dimensional world time is felt as circular, always returning, as in an eternal ritual.

Here the analyst would have to lend his mind, as the mother does in the primary relationship with her baby, until the analysand gives meaning to his emotions and represents them internally.

For Bion this is the realization of the preconception of the breast (the *thinking-breast* in the words of Meltzer, 1992), the first psychic preconception to be lived, realized, conceived, and represented.

Clinical examples: autistic children, children with disabilities and autistic manoeuvres, with a very poor or non-existent fantasy world (autistic, panic syndromes, nameless terrors). And these states can also be seen in psychotic analysands and even in neurotics.

States of partial relationship with the object (paranoid-schizoid position) represent the majority of cases, at times with transgenerational roots.

The predominant *anxieties* are paranoid, threatening to disintegrate the self. There is already a dissociation between good and bad objects, and the notion of self and the object as partial (mouth-breast).

Time is felt as oscillatory: going from the subject to the object and returning to the subject (mouth-breast-mouth). Space is three-dimensional, already with a notion of depth, the notion of interiority of self and of the object appears.

Projective identifications (the fantasy of projecting psychic elements from self into the object) predominate. In these states the subject already has a partial differentiation of the object (notion of mouth and breast), but feels like the centre of the world, as if everything revolves around his little "me" (*his majesty the baby* – Freud, 1914).

It is up to the analyst to invite the analysand to leave behind the predominance of the pleasure principle regime for that of the reality principle. To leave behind entrenched narcissism, often augmented by a pathological symbiosis where unlimited satisfaction is provided. The objects are partial: either idealized (extremely good) or denigrated (extremely bad). Tolerance of frustration generated by contact with reality is minimal.

These are children who often have an excess of material and academic care, but a deficit of affective-emotional care due to the lack of *reverie* (Bion, 1962) of the parental figures, who also function at the pre-genital level, and therefore do not has access to their own psychic singularity.

Here narcissistic disorders appear: phobias, hyperactivity (TDH), obsessive defences (OCD), with psychiatric diagnosis of bipolarity, and with all the symptoms arising from the lack of representation of internal and external reality, the lack of true contact with themselves, often resulting from a prolonged transgenerational pathological symbiosis.

Genital states (depressive position)

When the contact with total objects of internal and external reality predominates (accepting the good and bad of them). Object relations are of appreciation, reciprocity, solicitude and gratitude.

The world is felt as four-dimensional: with depth, and within a time that does not return. There is a notion of irreversible linear time, of object separation and capacity for mourning.

These children arrive for analysis when extreme situations occur in external or internal reality – when there is a major change in personal or school life, loss of a close relative, or at ages that require elaboration, such as adolescence.

Creative states – aesthetic position (Meltzer, 1984)

Using symbols resulting from singular and creative contact with internal and external reality.

When there are "flashes" of this position, it is a good prognosis: they are analysands who are "dreaming" and thinking reality in a particularly creative and singular way.

All of these states can alternate in the same analysis, sometimes in the same session. It is up to the analyst to observe their emergence after any formulation or interpretation given, so that they can adjust their communications to a level that is bearable in each moment for the analysand.

But a prior evaluation of the predominance of a new analysand's mental functioning can help greatly in the course of the analysis.

The analytical situation

The analytical situation is constituted of three elements, patient, analyst and setting, with which the analytical field is created (Baranger, 1969; Ferro, 1992; Ferro and Civitarese, 2015).

It is important to underline that each patient-analyst encounter is unique and takes place in the emotional contact between two minds within a consistent setting.

Clinical models

Freudian – the characters are understood as being part of relationships of the past history of the patient repeated in the transference.

Kleinian – the characters form part of a network of intra-psychical relationships that await a de-codification which clarifies their functioning originating from unconscious phantasies.

Bionian and Post-Bionian – the characters are co-generated in the present analytical situation forming part of an interpersonal narrative network.

> Through them, thanks to the analyst's alpha function (and that of the patient), protosensorialities and protoemotions are shared, narrated and transformed, gaining psychic representation, expanding mental containment and the personalities both of the patient and the analyst.

Dreaming emotional aspects is to contain them. If this does not take place the patient is destined to have physical symptoms, to act out, explode, control (hypo containment) or split (distancing undesirable aspects that may bring psychical pain).

All of these models for listening are always present and alternating in each analysis, even when we give priority to the Bionian model. Everything which takes place in the consultation within the analytical setting must arise, primordially, in the encounter between the singular qualities of the

> minds of *this* patient with *this* analyst in the field of the here-and-now of *this* session. As such, that which is transformed in the **current field** will then go back, transformed, to inhabiting the **inner world**, forming a **History** that will always be in transformation.
>
> (Di Chiara, 1992; cit. Ferro, 2007, p. 145)

The analytic session

In the analytic session two minds meet in the transience of life, and by being lived in each moment they co-produce dreams configured in play, drawings, and narration, derived from their daydreaming thought.

This work falls under the responsibility of the analyst, and in this sense the relationship with the analysand is asymmetrical. However, the relationship is symmetrical if we consider the value of the contributions of both minds.

It is essential for the analyst to have the capacity for *not-knowing* (a mind unsaturated, without memory, desire and understanding) in order to be in *unison* with the analysand (Bion, 1967), placed as close as possible to be able to provide formulations to the analysand that amplify thinkability (implicitly for the analyst too).

It is essential that the analyst listens to the signalling of the analysand's feelings of psychic proximity or distance from him, so that he can monitor the formulations he makes in the session to open up paths for growth.

Dreaming in the session

Here I will present clinical vignettes of a boy with autistic defences: the first at the beginning of the analysis, and the second after a year and a half. They mark steps in the construction and amplification of psychic containment and dreaming-thinking.

Max

Despite his school recommending psychological evaluation from the age of 3, Max only comes for analysis at the age of 6 with a diagnosis of autism made by a child neurologist. He is blond, tall for his age, wears glasses with thick lenses, and walks stooped forward looking towards the ground. He enters, glances up at me and smiles, then goes back to looking at the ground. He sits on the floor, folds over the rug so his legs are touching the floorboards (he´s wearing shorts), takes all the coloured pencils from the box and places them side by side on the floor. He rolls the pencils together on the floor and imitates the sound they make, singing happily (Haudenschild, 2002, 2015).

Through his primitive play (*autistic manoeuvres* – Tustin, 1981), expressing joy, and the glance and smile he gave me when he arrived, I intuit that he is grateful to be here.

I then introduce a modification to his "play": I place a yellow pencil upright and "march" tapping it on the floor, singing – "I am Max. I´m going to the barracks!" He immediately takes a red pencil and tries to stand it up, saying "Mummy". Taking his hand, I make the red pencil march while I move the Max-pencil, singing: "Mummy and Max are going to the barracks!"

He laughs and puts the dark green pencil beside Mummy, and I sing: "Daddy is going to the barracks with Mummy and Max!" And I tap the Daddy-pencil louder on the floor. Then he stands the orange pencil up and points to me and I say: "Teresa, Mummy, Daddy and Max are going to the barracks!" He laughs while we move the pencils, hitting them loudly on the floor, each one with a different rhythm and force. He then lifts up the light green pencil and says: "Bobby" (brother), the pink pencil: "Rose", (sister) the black pencil, and says: "Ee-Ee". I say: "Peter" (his driver who is black), and he chuckles, as if thanking me for being understood. Max repeats this play at the beginning of the sessions.

Max also blows bubbles of saliva and he draws this saliva out from his mouth towards me (he has allergic rhinitis). I point out that these beautiful bubbles, this "water" that comes from inside him, is like the water that comes from my tap, and we can play with it. He asks me to turn on the tap, but I take his hand and help him do it. I put little paper boats in the sink, and he puts pencils in pairs inside them: him and Mummy, Daddy and Bobby, Teresa and Rose, pairs that he changes while I sing and move the boats around on the water, like on a Sunday afternoon (Beadell and Tollerton, 1946). I substitute the pencils for dolls and make them move around too, and he plays like this often until one day he puts Daddy sitting on the tap observing the boats, and people diving, swimming and having fun in the water.

This capacity to observe from a distance and see oneself implies the introjection and formation of mental space capable of containing, observing and receiving experiences.

Every time he adds a variation, I sing something different, such as: "There goes Max on a trip with Mummy!" Then: "Daddy and Bobby want to drive too! . . .

Rose and Teresa have to come along too! . . . Now Max is going to swim with Bobby and dive in Teresa's water". I accompany each of his variations with a rhythmic and sung verbalization, always in the same melody.

Through the animation and interrelation of the objects, Max's dreaming-thinking can open up its own paths.

Max's dreaming-thinking

Drawings: affective holograms

Drawing what Max asked me to was extremely fruitful in our work together (see Figure 6.2). All of this began one day when he arrived with dried snot on his face (he has rhinitis which worsens when he has a cold) and I comment: "you

Figure 6.2

look like Smudge!"[4] (his pencil case had a Smudge design) and he asked me to wipe his face. I took a tissue, wet it under the tap, and cleaned his face. He took his drawing book and asked me to draw Smudge in it.

Then he took a tissue and cleaned Smudge's face on the drawing. Next, he asked me to draw a clean Smudge and showed me his clean face and smiled. Then I drew him beside Smudge, cleaning Smudge's face.

Drawing little scenes and including him in them, allows him to see himself there and store this in his mind. His drawing book serves as a place where these scenes can have continuity, even though they are modified in each session. Sometimes he arrives and the first thing he does is to leaf through his drawing book, stopping at certain scenes and showing me them, as if wanting to check that I share this memory, as proof of their reality.

In Max's search for characters, these drawings are *affective holograms* (Ferro, 1992) of relationships between people, "syncretically naming" emotions and therefore allowing for the development of increasingly complex narratives related to them.

Max now constructs little scenes himself with the toys and asks me to draw them in his book. Each scene I draw is interpreted based on the affective relational context in that moment. Introjected as visual snapshots, these representations broaden the subject's visual-dreaming capacity.

The boy who could hardly distinguish between inanimate objects now has access to his thinking-dreaming, to his human existence.

Intuitive comprehension and shifts towards progression

In the first meeting with Max, although he does not verbalize, I intuit his gratitude and capacity to live more healthily, based on the joy with which he receives the objects from the toy box and uses them, and also in the way he receives my associations and the play I introduce.

Given the almost total absence of verbal communication, intuition was fundamental to listening and the analytical dialogue.

The autistic manoeuvres (rolling the pencils and drawing out his saliva) give way to the play that I propose, and he accepts, in each opportune moment, in the here and now of each session, (Joseph, 1989). His solitary play (he lived confined to the third floor of his house, without participating in family life) transforms into shared play, in live company (Alvarez, 1992): with me, at home with his siblings (who I invited to a meeting without him), and his school colleagues.

The part of his personality that has been maintained outside of human relational contact now gives more space to the healthy part, that can participate in relational life with the family, school colleagues and even neighbours, seeking out and getting closer to those who he intuits are more receptive to him and who resonate emotionally.

Notes

1 "Caminante, no hay camino, se hace camino al andar. Al andar se hace el camino, y al volver la vista atrás se ve la senda que nunca se ha de volver a pisar".
2 And with an unsaturated mind, without memory, desire, and understanding.
3 Constitutive steps towards human speech for Heidegger.
4 A Brazilian cartoon character who was always dirty and didn't like to bathe.

References

Alvarez, A. (1992). *Live Company: Psychoanalytic Psychotherapy with Autistic, Border-line, Deprived, and Abused Children*. London: Tavistock-Routledge.
Baranger, M.E.W. (1969). La situación analítica como campo dinámico. In *Problemas del campo psicoanalítico*. Buenos Aires: Kargieman.
Beadell, E., and Tollerton, N. (1946). *Cruising Down the River*. New York: Columbia Records.
Bion, W. (1962). A Theory of Thinking. *International Journal of Psychology*, 43: 305–310.
Bion, W. (1967). *Second Thoughts*. London: Heinemann.
Di Chiara, G. (1992). L'incontro, il racconto, il commiato. Tre fatori fondamentali dell'esperienza psicoanalitica. In *L'esperienza condivisa*. Milano: Rafaello Cortina.
Ferro, A. (1992). *La tecnica nella psicoanalisi infantile*. Milano: Rafaello Cortina.
Ferro, A. (2002). *Seeds of Illness, Seeds of Recovery: The Genesis of Suffering and the Role of Psychoanalysis*. Great Britain: Brunner-Routledge, 2005.
Ferro, A. (2003). *The Bi-Personal Field: Experiences in Child Analysis*. London: Routledge.
Ferro, A. (2007). *Evitare le emozioni, vivere le emozioni*. Milano: Raffaello Cortina. (Como está en la bibliografia. Em português seria: (2011). Evitar as emoções, viver as emoções. Porto Alegre: Artmed.) Por favor, cambie el año en el texto.
Ferro e Civitarese. (2015). *Il campo analitico e le sue transformazioni*. Milano: Rafaello Cortina.
Freud , S. (1914) Remembering, repeting, and working-trough S.E., 12 147–156
Haudenschild, T. (2002). Utilizzazione dela capacità di reverie dell'analista, del gioco attivo e del disegno: opzioni techniche nell'analisi di bambini che non comunicano verbalmente. In *Quaderni di Psicoterapia Infantile*. Vol. 45, pp. 118–131.
Haudenschild, T. (2015). *O primeiro olhar: desenvolvimento psíquico inicial, déficit e autismo*. São Paulo: Escuta.
Heidegger, M. (1927). *L'être et le temps*. Paris: Gallimard, 1972.
Heidegger, M. (1954). *L'experience de la pensée*. Paris: Gallimard, 1966.
Joseph, B. (1989). *Psychic Equilibrium and Psychici Change*. London: Routledge.
Kant, I. (1787). *Crítica da Razão Pura*, 3a ed. São Paulo: Nova Cultural, 1999.
Machado, A. (1912). Fragmento XXIX de Proverbios y Cantares: Campos de Castilla. In *Poesias Completas*. Madrid: Espasa Calpe.
Meltzer, D. (1975). *Explorations in Autism*. Perthshire: Clunie Press.
Meltzer, D. (1984). Sulla bidimensionalità. In *Quaderni di Psicoterapia Infantile*. Roma: Borla.
Meltzer, D. (1992). Além da consciência. In *Revista Brasileira de Psicanálise*. Vol. 26, n. 3, pp. 397–408.
Merleau-Ponty, M. (1969). *La prose du monde*. Paris: Gallimard.
Mitrani, J. (2001). *Ordinary People and Extra-ordinary Protections: A Post-kleinian Approach to the Treatment of Primitive Mental States*. Great Britain: Brunner Routledge.
Tustin, F. (1981). *Autistic States in Children*. London: Routledge.

Chapter 7

Intuition and analyst language
A language of emotion

Celia Fix Korbivcher

> Just as the archaeologist has to be very careful when he thinks he has reached some potentially revealing object and has to resort not to a spade or a shovel but a camel-hair brush, so the analyst has to know when to discard these crude and violent methods and when to pick up something far gentler, far more revealing and less destructive than a shovel.
>
> (Bion, 1997, p. 26)

The proposal to analyze patients with predominant manifestations of the primordial mind may seem paradoxical. I refer specifically to neurotic patients with autistic nuclei (Tustin, 1986). Such individuals avoid closeness and intimacy and are terrified of establishing contact with others. They are patients who acquire intellectual knowledge about how relationships should be and imitate what would be a contact between two individuals, without experiencing the corresponding emotion. They understand that they must relate, that they need to get out of isolation, but for them, the awareness of the bodily separation from the object is intolerable and causes intense experiences of unintegration, threat of falling into an endless space, and dissolution and dilution. As a way of avoiding such states, these individuals isolate themselves within a protective shell in which they remain absorbed in autistic auto-sensual maneuvers. This is the scenario that we find while working with primordial mental states – unintegrated and autistic states. From my point of view, these states are close to what Bion (1997) called "inaccessible states of mind," embryonic states accompanied by sub-thalamic manifestations of fear, an area that relates to the area of unintegrated phenomena.[1]

I question, how is it possible for the analyst to have access to such inaccessible states of mind in order to enable the patient to become aware of them, contain them in his mind, and transform them into thought? How can the analyst identify and attribute meaning to communications that he perceives as having no trace of psychic traits? How to exercise the capacity of "reverie" and alpha function in the face of such experiences? What language should the analyst use to communicate with primordial states of mind – unintegrated and autistic states in his cultured and developed patients? (Korbivcher, 2016a)

DOI: 10.4324/9781003293385-8

My purpose in this work is to examine what tools the analyst has available to work with neurotic patients who operate with primordial mental states. I develop ideas about the functioning of the primordial mind and investigate the type of language that the analyst must use to communicate with unintegrated states, with the autistic barriers of these patients, in order to favor some contact. I suggest that this language would be the language of emotion (Korbivcher, 2017), a language analogous to the model of the motherese prosody of the mother with her baby. I suggest that this kind of language would be an experience that relates to the notion of transformations in O (Bion, 1965). Finally, I present a clinical material in order to illustrate the issues addressed in this work to enable a discussion.

Primordial mind

The term "primordial mind," according to Green (1998), is not so clear at first glance. It is based on its opposition to the "civilized, individual, educated, and articulated" parts of the human being.

According to Green (1998),

> Bion relates [the primordial mind] to some sort of imaginary embryology of the mind. Bion shares a common hypothesis with Freud that there is something primitive in the mind that is not entirely explained by the early stages of object relationships in the development of the baby. The traces left by phylogenesis and ontogenesis in the structure of the mind should play a significant role in later stages of development. . . . The primordial mind is made up of thoughts which, because of their raw and crude nature, are not workable as such. So they have to be expelled from the psyche. The destiny of thoughts produced by a thinker is to be kept in the mind and continue to be transformed into mental abstractions.
>
> (p. 651)

Green also questions,

> How can a thought without a thinker be expelled from the mind, considering that the discharge process sends them out of the mind and does not carry with it the whole of the primitive mental activity? The probable answer is that it is impossible to get rid entirely of the β-elements that stay blocked in the mind and will poison other mental processes if they gain the upper hand again.
>
> (p. 651)

This means that the mind contains unborn embryonic remnants that have not been transformed and that remain present even in neurotic individuals' minds throughout their lives. Bion's emphasis on the primordial mind favors the individual to recognize these manifestations without representation, navigate through them, and eventually transform them into some meaning, enabling them to be thought and named.

In his clinical practice, the analyst should ask, at each movement in the session, who is the patient he is meeting with and at what mental level he is operating, whether on a neurotic, psychotic, or primordial level – autistic and unintegrated. The rules that operate on neurotic or psychotic levels are completely different from those that operate on primordial levels. Patients wrapped in unintegrated states lack the notion of a limit capable of keeping emotional content together, resulting in lack of discrimination between internal and bodily substances. Bodily manifestations without mental representation prevail. It will be from the introjection of an external object continuously interacting with the baby's body surface that a psychic skin will form, giving rise to the fantasies of internal and external space. If for some reason, the primary skin function is disturbed, a second skin will develop to prevent the baby from living intolerable unintegrated experiences. This is a protective maneuver with autistic characteristics. Unlike grouped alpha and beta elements, which give rise to contact barriers and beta screen, respectively, and grouped autistic elements, which give rise to autistic barriers, grouped unintegrated elements do not produce any type of barrier, they rather spread and disperse (Korbivcher, 2016a).

Faced with autistic barriers and unintegrated states, the analyst is unable to find in his repertoire an adequate language to access and transform such experiences from the patient in order to reach him. The analyst's capacity of reverie and alpha function is inoperable since such patients are in a non-mentalized state in which their capability to dream is obstructed. The presence of the other separated individual is not perceived as such. The relationship is established through sensation objects – autistic objects and autistic shapes (Tustin, 1986) – by the sensations provoked by contact and not by fantasies and emotions that could be aroused.

For the analyst to reach such patients, the autistic barrier must acquire some porosity to provide access to that frozen area. This would be the analyst's task; at first, to penetrate the autistic barrier – this inanimate and lifeless world – to bring its content to life and give it some meaning. But the question is: how can one penetrate the autistic barrier and make it more permeable or even dissolve it?

When facing patients with predominant autistic states, the analyst himself is exposed to experiences of non-existence. This experience is difficult to bear and requires him to operate with his negative capability (Bion, 1970). For the analyst to penetrate the patient's autistic barrier, he (the analyst) needs to use the same sensory language of the patient as a mean of creating a sensorial link between both. This experience would favor the patient to feel less threatened in the presence of the analyst – a separate person – and eventually encourage the patient to abandon his autistic maneuvers in order to initiate a protocommunication between them.

Faced with unintegrated states, the analyst being himself in unison with the patient's unintegrated mental state "becomes" that experience, and by containing it in his mind, he is eventually able to bring together those scattered elements. The analyst's capacity of reverie and alpha function may then operate. The content that was previously frozen within the autistic barrier, or spread out, becomes now accessible to the analyst, allowing him to dream it and eventually give it some meaning. What were once unintegrated and autistic elements now become beta elements that can be transformed into alpha elements by the action of the alpha function. The patient, from various experiences such as these, may feel encouraged to share human experiences involving the tolerance of mental pain and suffering, without the feeling of such vulnerability.

The language of the analyst

Verbal language is the main mean of communication in the analyst's work. Words are what will transform the emotional experience into alpha elements enabling the experience to be thought. However, words can be revealing or concealing, depending on the type of ongoing emotion. Words can even become a real obstacle in the communication. Nonverbal language, in turn, often translates the emotion of the moment more accurately than words. The analyst's intuition and imagination will be the elements that will prevail in the process of choosing the language that he will use with his patient (Chuster, 2016 personal communication); Korbivcher (2016a).

Mothers, as we know, use the motherese prosody to communicate with their babies. This kind of language attracts the baby to the contact.

According to Laznik (2013), the motherese is characterized by

A voice register that is louder than usual, a restricted intonation range but with modulations and variations in height . . . Research indicates that this type of prosody is a carrier of affective information for the newborn. For the adult who addresses the baby, it is a source of pleasure. The quality of this prosody is a co-creation of the pair, *i.e.*, it depends on the baby's participation.

(p. 94)

According to Annie Reiner (2012), babies demonstrate curiosity and feel attracted to communications conveying emotion. The author quotes Norman (2004), who says: "infants read facial expressions and understand emotional meaning when there is a concordance between the lexical (verbal) and non-lexical (sounds, intonations, gestures) aspects of the spoken language" (p. 34).

In the maternal motherese prosody, the rhythm and musicality of the voice are essential elements in the communication.

As Trewarthen and Gratier 2005 said:

The spontaneous musicality of verbal language is as significant as the words, and it is from this type of language that shared subjective experiences will occur. The voice is, for the baby, a fundamental expressive instrument, and it will be from the variations of the musical rhythm of this proto-conversation that the baby will build his or her relationship with others.

(Trewarthen and Gratier, 2005; apud Laznik, 2013. p. 98)

This means that in the motherese prosody, what is relevant is not the content and meaning of the words used by the mother with the baby, but rather, its prosody. The emotion of the mother is translated by the rhythm and intonation of her voice, her facial expression, her muscle tone when carrying the baby, etc. This kind of language will call up the baby to the contact with the mother. From that moment on, an interaction initiates between mother and baby linked by a "language of emotion," a language in which both become the emotion of the moment.

I suggest that the communication between mother and baby occurring from the motherese prosody is a model close to Bion's notion of transformations in O (1965).

The transformation in O is an experience in progress that promotes important psychic changes in the patient. It emerges at a certain moment in the session to be recognized and experienced. Transformation in K, on the other hand, relates to an experience that has already happened and is known to some extent (Vermote, 2011).

Faced with transformation into O, patient and analyst being in unison with each other share a common emotional experience. This is a true meeting moment in which both become the emotion of the moment. The language that promotes experiences of this nature is, as I am proposing, the "language of emotion" (Korbivcher, 2016a),

Bion (1970) suggested the notion of "language of success" based on Keats's idea of a "Man of Achievement:" "negative capability, that is, when a man is capable of being in uncertainties, mysteries, doubts, without any irritable reaching after fact and reason." In my opinion, the "language of emotion" is independent of the use of negative capability; it stems from a contact between the pair in which both become the emotion of the moment, and I think that this is the experience that could actually allow communication.

Clinical material

Pedro is a tall, handsome 20-year-old young man. His grassy hair is very long sometimes covering his face. The absence of life and emotion in his expression and a lack of care about his appearance are noteworthy. He speaks very softly, and one can hardly understand what he says. In our first contact, Pedro informs me that he came to seek analysis at the suggestion of his family because he is a very closed person and does not talk to people. He says he is very quiet and only speaks when requested, and that once the subject is exhausted, the conversation does not continue. He talks only with his twin brother and two close friends. He says that he spends most of his time in his bedroom, involved with his iPad, listening to music, watching series, and sometimes playing an instrument.

A session

Pedro comes in with his lifeless, slack way, extends his limp hand, and sits on the edge of the couch. He looks at me and, in a ritualistic way, informs without any emotion that he had no class, and that he studied in the morning and exercised at home. He smiles and says, as if his task was over: "That's it!" He remains silent, drumming his fingers rhythmically. When asked what he was thinking about, he responds: "Nothing!" He is silent for a while and then looks at me and says, with an inquisitive expression: "I have nothing to talk about! Nothing that could be interesting!" I say that perhaps he could talk about what he thinks that could not be interesting. Maybe that could be of interest. He says he had not done anything today and that yesterday he was there with me. I feel disheartened by the difficulty of establishing contact. I even think about proposing to Pedro to cut down one session, in an attempt, perhaps, to try to minimize my suffering in that situation, but I say nothing and decide to wait. After some time, he repeats, using the same tone, that he got up in the morning, studied, exercised, and then waited for the time to come here, took the car and came singing along the way, as always. I say, Ah! Did you sing on your way here? And what songs did you sing? He says, a Blues! It occurs to me that I also like to sing and usually do that in the car. I notice an opportunity to establish a communication. I talk about singing in the car and ask if he sings in the shower. He says that he does not, that the singing is not for others to hear. I mention that coming to the session seems to make him happy, that it brings him a good feeling. It immediately occurs to me to ask if he would like to sing to me the song that he sang in the car. He becomes surprised and refuses, embarrassed. I also become surprised and somewhat uncomfortable about the pertinence of the proposal, but I decide to go ahead. I playfully tell him that if he prefers, I can cover my face, so I don't see him singing. I say that I, too, could also sing a song. He ends up agreeing, sits on the edge of the couch and very seriously starts singing. I become astonished with his beautiful very deep voice and with his seriousness while singing. I comment on his voice and question about the lyrics. I ask him to repeat the lyrics.

He says:

> I hurt myself today to see if I still feel. I focus on the pain, the only thing that is real. The needle tears a hole, the old familiar sting. Try to kill it all, but I remember everything. What have I become, my sweetest friend! Everyone I know goes away in the end.

I am impacted by the content of the lyrics. I ask him what he thinks about it and he says: "It's a sad song." He . . . moved away from a turbulent past to feel nothing. He smiles and says: "I think that you would say that it has to do with me." I answer, jokingly: "Me? You are the one who is saying that. What would it have to do with you?"

He says the song is about a person who had a turbulent past, got hurt, and lost his feelings. He continues, "He ends up hurting others and is alone in the end."

Me: "I wonder how would that have to do with you?"

Him: "It has to do with distance, that I don't talk much, about feelings, about numbing myself."

I ask, "But what about your past?"

Him: "I don't know, but I don't think there's much for me to try to forget."

I say that by proposing that he sings, I had said that I would also sing because this could also be a kind of communication, like the one that was happening there. He asks me to sing. I feel disconcerted and resist. But then I notice that a mood of intimacy had been created between us, and I end up agreeing. I sing a short aria by Mozart: "Voi que sapete." He listens to me surprised and interested. He says that he doesn't know operas.

I say: "You have been very numb. The song you sang talks about someone who needs to get hurt to feel that he exists."

I ask why he needs to become numb.

Him: "In order not to be in the spotlight, the more closed I am, the less I appear. But this can be bad too, because I would be missing out on a new experience."

I say: "So would this be your wound?"

Him: "It's a way of hurting myself; everything becomes more robotic, not human!"

I say: "Robots do not feel pain, but they do not feel pleasure either."

He says: "They don't feel anything!"

I say playfully: "So, you said at first that you had nothing to say, how is it now?" I say that he seems to have enjoyed singing here and listening to me. I say that he took a risk and sang, and with that, lived something new here that he never lived before and, therefore, we had a new, pleasant, living experience. I add that if he had been numb, like the character of the song, none of this would have happened. I tell him that he does not have to hurt himself to "feel," that he felt a lot of emotions here today without having to hurt himself.

The mood in the session becomes very intense. I find myself enveloped by the experience we both went through, a true encounter, very meaningful for both of us. The session ends and upon leaving, Pedro extends firmly his hand and says: "Thank you!" I ask him what he was thankful about, if it had to do with what we experienced there. He confirms and leaves.

Comments

As we can see, Pedro operates predominantly with important primordial manifestations – autistic nuclei. His lifeless expression, distant look, flabby hands, low voice, and finger tapping, along with his silence and withdrawal in the sessions are indicative of this state. The long, kind of greasy hair covering his face resembles a mask that protects him from the presence of others. At any initiative of contact, the analyst is faced with this insurmountable mask/barrier. For Pedro, the awareness of the separate presence of the other person is threatening and terrifying, leading him to isolation and protection. With this, Pedro distances himself from the human world to live in a lifeless, lonely, deserted world, in order to avoid any intimate contact with others.

How can we think about what would have favored Pedro to come out of isolation and communicate his terrors to the analyst in the last fragment presented?

What language would the analyst have used to approach Pedro and enabled him to have contact not only with others but also with himself?

Music is a sound element present since the beginning of Pedro's analysis. This is the sensory pathway that allows him to communicate with the analyst, although at many moments, music also operates as a protective barrier against the vulnerability caused by the conscience of the analyst as a separate person. With music, Pedro acquires a state of greater cohesion, some contour that guarantees him the notion of the sense of existence at a physical level. To approach Pedro and penetrate his autistic barrier, the analyst uses Pedro's own sensory way, and through that, she transforms the elements that compose the autistic barrier into a mean of communication between the pair. By doing that, the analyst summons Pedro out of his isolation. Being in unison with Pedro's emotional state and seeing him unable to communicate, the analyst suggests him to sing the song he was singing in his car on his way to the session. This communication would be what I call a "language of emotion"; the analyst becoming the ongoing emotion. The analyst's gesture demonstrating availability and interest in listening to Pedro conveys to him her emotion – continence, embrace – far from words and reason. In this way, music loses its character of an autistic barrier and becomes a vehicle of emotional communication between the pair. We must remember that the analyst also sings a song for Pedro, thus providing a relationship of greater intimacy between both. This experience triggers a mood in which analyst and patient become the emotion at play. From then on, Pedro can communicate with words his terrors expressed in the lyrics ("I hurt myself today to see if I still feel . . ."), which were frozen within the autistic barrier. With her capacity of reverie and alpha function, the analyst gives meaning to Pedro's communication. I propose that this experience comes close to the notion of transformations in

$O \rightarrow K$ (Bion, 1965).

Finally, it is important to mention that when Pedro meets the analyst at the beginning of the session, he extends his limp hand and says he has nothing to say. However, upon leaving, Pedro says goodbye, firmly shakes the analyst's hand, and says "thank you," referring to the experience that he had at the session. We might think that Pedro appreciated the rare opportunity of sharing a living experience with the analyst without feeling so threatened.

In conclusion, I point out that the analyst facing transformations in O shares with the patient an intense emotional experience in which a true mood of great intimacy prevails beyond words, an experience that can only be lived and cannot be known. This experience, as I suggested, has the same characteristics of the language of the motherese prosody of the mother with her baby. The emotion transmitted by the mother is the main element that enables the emotional contact with the baby. We can say, then, that the analyst must be attentive to the choice of language that he will use with his patient, and that the language is an essential element in establishing true emotional contact between the pair.

As Bion (1997) wrote, "Psycho-analysis needs to be carefully done, because the situation is so precarious and because it is so difficult to find the minimum conditions for achieving wisdom either in oneself or in . . . the patient" (Bion, 1997, p. 26).

Note

1 The phenomenon of unintegration (Bick, 1968) is characterized by the absence of the notion of a limit capable of holding emotional contents together, resulting in lack of discrimination between internal and bodily substances. It will be from the introjection of an external object continuously interacting with the surface of the baby's body that a psychic skin will form giving rise to the fantasies of internal and external spaces. If for some reason the function of the primary skin is disturbed, a second skin develops to protect the baby from intolerable experiences of unintegration.

References

Bick, E. (1968). The Experience of the Skin in the Early Object- Relations. *The International Journal of Psychoanalysis*, 49: 484–486.
Bion, W.R. (1965). *Transformations*. London: Karnac, 1984.
Bion, W.R. (1970). *Attention and Interpretation*. London: Karnac, 1984.
Bion, W.R. (1997). *Taming Wild Thoughts*. London: Karnac
Green, A. (1998). The Primordial Mind and the Work of the Negative. *The International Journal of Psychoanalysis*, 79: 649–665.
Korbivcher, C.F. (2016a). *Emotion, Non- Emotion and Analyst Language*. Italia: Koinos, 2017.
Korbivcher, F.C. (2016b). The Analyst's Mind, Theories, and Transformations in "O". In A. Reiner (Ed.), *Of Things Invisible to Mortal Sight: Celebrating the Work of James Grotstein*. London: Karnac.
Laznik, M.C. (2013). Linguagem e comunicação do bebê até 3 meses. In *O bebê e seus intérpretes: clínica e pesquisa Laznik M. C. e Cohen D. organizadores)*. Instituto Langage, p. 94.
Reiner, A. (2012). *Bion and Being: Passion and Creative Mind*. London: Karnac.
Tustin, F. (1986). *Autistic Barriers in Neurotic Patients*. London: Karnac, 2012.
Vermote, R. (2011). On the Value of "Late Bion" to Analytic Theory and Practicy. *The International Journal of Psychoanalysis*, 92(5): 1089–1098.

Chapter 8

The mystical experience in search of a session

Jani Santamaría Linares

While the eyes are the ones that see, the mind does the observing.
(José Saramago)

Wilfred Bion's school of thought has become an integral part of the psycho-analytic common core (Blass, 2012), and his contributions are the most-widely quoted in psychoanalytic theory (Levine, 2019). The originality of his ideas and the new models he proposed are enriching, extensive, and have paved the way for new treatment perspectives; especially as far as acute pathologies are concerned. However, his attention was not only limited to pathologies, but he also explored mental health matters, such as his definition of the vital and creative mind (Reiner, 2016; Santamaría, 2016). Because of the wide scope of his thinking, I wondered about the need to discuss what some authors have called "the late Bion" (Blean-donu, 1994; Vermote, 2010), especially the "O" concept.

Bion (1970) defines the "O" as follows:

> I shall use the letter "O" to denote that which is the ultimate reality, described with phrases such the absolute truth, the infinite, the divinity, the thing in itself. . . . It can "become," but it cannot be "known." It is darkness and formlessness . . . but it enters the domain of K when it has evolved to a point where it can be known, through knowledge gained by experience, and formu-lated in terms derived from sensuous experience; its existence is conjectured phenomenologically.
>
> (1970, p. 26)

According to the "no memory, no desire" clinical attitude he proposed in 1967, Aguayo (2019) stated that Bion changed his clinical approach from a "tendency to excessively pathologize the patient to one of acknowledging the importance of the analyst's subjectivity and alpha function" (p. 5). The analytical process is seen as an ever-growing spiral of changes in "K" (knowledge) and transformations in "O" (Santamaría, 2018).

DOI: 10.4324/9781003293385-9

In my opinion, all of the previously mentioned contributions represent a paradigm shift in which Bion placed "mysticism" center stage of the contemporary psychoanalytic activity. The present work attempts to define the mystical (intuitive) state, from the perspective of W. Bion conversing with Freud. It is my intention to shed light on such processes, by clinically presenting my emotional experience with Elsa.

The mystical phenomenon has been the object of psychoanalytic study and reflection by several authors: Bergstein (2018), Botella (1989/2003), Tauzsik (2011), Vermote (2012), Levine (2018), etc. All of them have reflected upon the role this subject plays within our discipline. Generally speaking, there is a consensus with Bion's idea that mysticism and the "O" (ultimate reality in everlasting transit) oppose the religious viewpoint; because it is the uncertainty and desire to learn about the "O" what encourages a questioning and reflection of the experience, so that one can learn from it.

The "formal" beginning of Bion as a "mystical analyst" was presented by Vermote (2011), who believes that the "late Bion" also provided a theoretical and practical contribution. He states that it is possible to combine both models, differentiating them as "the first" and the "late Bion," to construct a two-track system in search of psychic change" (p. 93).

Levine (2011) believes that the "O" may be regarded as related to the universe of the unfathomable. It is intimately connected to the clinical centrality and pursuit of the psychoanalytic object, along with the analyst's need to achieve a state of "reverie" (p. 331).

Grotstein (2000) reinforces the idea of a mystical Bion in several of his articles, in which he recounts that when he was in therapy with him, he heard him say: "The analyst, instead of listening to the patient, should listen to himself listening to the patient." This is how Bion introduced the mystical vertex in psychoanalysis for the first time, as a brand-new technique (p. 105).

The term "mystical" denotes vague and opaque associations, some of which are negative if considered to be a pathological manifestation, and not a mental state of geniality. In *Attention and Interpretation* (1970), Bion describes a concept called "mystical mentality"; which is the capacity of receiving creative thoughts, to the extent in which one is receptive to thoughts without a thinker.

For many years, science and mysticism have been considered separate matters. But this biased approach has limited the richness and seriousness the subject requires. "Scientific" is associated with the idea that "only the things that can be seen, exist"; while the word mystical refers to the unknown.

W. Bion asserted that, thanks to our verbal capacity, there is a certain domain of our mental life that we can describe in terms of personality, mind, etc. However, it is only a small part of the spectrum that can be communicated, verbally. In the psychoanalytic encounter, we are forced to observe and figure out other areas of the mind beyond that limited sphere. As Bion said: "The ultimate reality must be a whole, even if the human animal is unable to understand it" (Bion, 1977, p. 229). In our practice, we find ourselves in the realm of what is invisible to the senses but known intuitively; something Bergstein (2018) called "*juxtaposition between analytic thought and mysticism*" (p. 7).

In 1929, S. Freud defined the mystical experience in a dialog he had with author Romain Rolland, in the overture of *Civilization and its Discontents* (1930). Responding to Rolland's proposal of differentiating between religion and religiousness (as a sense of boundless eternity), Freud created the hypothesis of an *Undifferentiated Self* that remains latent and operating within the adult. Originally, this "Self" contained everything, but was later segregated in the outer world (1929, p. 68). At that moment, he defined it as an "oceanic feeling," as a return to the narcissistic fusion of the first months of life, where the limits between the Self and the outer world were blurred. In 1938, he revisited the idea and wrote: "*Mysticism is the obscure perception of the Self, of the realm that is outside the Ego, the Id*" (Freud, 1938b, p. 302).

The former is useful in the understanding of the area that I wish to discuss, related to Bion's redefinition of the concept "free-floating attention" (1970), originally coined by Freud (1912). The English author wrote that the analyst's mental state approached something akin to what Freud described in his letter to Salome in 1916: "*I know that my work has artificially blinded me to concentrate all the light into a dark passageway.*"

He claimed that psychoanalysts should use their intuition to keep the remembrances from being tampered with by intrusion or the desire to understand. The more the analyst is freed from that and is permanently disciplined, the more certain he will be that his observations are not originally stemming from his personal equation (1992, pp. 264–265).

He added that, in his experience with the use of this process, the intuition of a "present evolution" is enabled, and future ones are given a steppingstone. According to him, the psychoanalytical attitude "*is a deliberate act that depends on the active suspension of memory and desire: it is a work model that invites the analyst and the patient to commit to an emotional experience that captures the sparks of the unknowable*" (1970).

In 1970, he described it as:

> The ability of the analyst to reach "blindness" is a prerequisite to "see" the evolved elements of the "O." In reciprocity, his freedom to be "blinded" by the sensory-based qualities (or his perception of them) must allow him to "see" the aspects evolving from the O that are invariant to the subject.
>
> (p. 59)

An "artificial blindness" demonstrates a listening that is not worried about perceptible elements and thus, can notice things that are not sensory-based. According to Category C of Bion's Grid (1965), we can say that the "analyst is a mystic in search of truth, and he pursues emotional veracity even in the disturbed areas, allowing patients to acquire a knowledge that enrichens their personalities" (Santamaría, 2018).

As we can see, Bion placed concepts that are little studied by psychoanalysis center stage, and his theoretical formulations started and ended up with the analysis. He always tried to prepare our minds for the encounter with the patient. Following suit, I will now present a clinical vignette in which I will lay out mystical experiences in the sessions' encounters.

Clinical vignette

Elsa was a 32-year-old professional who started psychoanalysis due to her desire to help her 8-year-old son. I found a very pretty woman in front of me, with a sad look in her eyes, and very much concerned about her physical appearance. She felt afraid of living, and described her life as "dry" and "mechanical." She was well schooled and cultivated, part of a high economic status. She did not have a job; and had a tendency to procrastinate her tasks and commitments. She had had a brother, six years older than her, who had committed suicide; and whom she described as her mom's favorite. She got married with the illusion of giving her parents the joy of a grandchild. She dreaded questioning her marriage, and there was a predominant feeling of guilt for her feeling a chronic apathy, and for sensing her mothering abilities were not good enough.

During the first interview, she reported:

> During a conference, you spoke of a patient who had no sexual life. You used the metaphor of a house, and you said that living that way, was like living in a house in which one of the rooms – the kitchen – was never used. I remember that because that is exactly how I feel: I live in a house (a life), but I barely use any of the rooms. I could very well live without sex, since that room of "the house" has been locked for many years.

Elsa was constantly on a diet. Her ideal of not having "a single ounce of fat" also applied to her mental functioning: "not a single ounce of conflict." She wished to produce an ascetic ideal in which the most important mandate was to reduce all desire to its minimum expression.

She presented herself as a mind devoid of curiosity. Her bonds were deprived of the fertile and vital capacity to connect ideas and emotions, and to generate potential thoughts that could support her sense of vitality. In Bion's (1970) own words: "*She experienced pain, but not suffering*" (p. 87). This meant that Elsa interpreted pain as something that was inflicted upon her, not as an experience that she ran into. According to Goldiuk (2018), "*suffering* makes reference to the intimate and emotional encounter with ourselves. It evokes finitude and our primordial loneliness."

During our first meetings, Elsa seemed to experience feelings of futility, emptiness and stagnation. She told me she would not speak of her childhood because she did not remember it; and because it had been a "normal" one. She seemed to be "frozen" in an overly dramatic "now" that extended forever.

In the beginning, and for many months in a row, the analysis would take place in a thirty or twenty-minute span, because Elsa would arrive late and give excuses for her tardiness, such as the distance, traffic, etc. Some obsessive traits hindered our work, especially the intellectualization that prevented her from contacting her own emotions. When the fear of being abandoned by her husband started to be broached, she would increase her hypochondriac obsessions. She had actually undergone several minor surgeries, and she recounted some asthma episodes as a child that "disappeared on their own." She seemed to accept my casual observations, but the ambiance was usually tense, due to her constant threat of suspending the analysis at any moment. My participation was more active, since she would ask questions and I would follow them as echoes that tried to give her voice back to her own narrative.

Her constant absence (the "incomplete" sessions) started having a concerning effect on me, since several thoughts were starting to "filter" in. I realized I was feeling less and less curious about what was happening. I got an urge to "condition" her treatment to her punctuality, and I would discover myself with the desire of telling her: "If you do not get here on time, we will stop." I did, however, acknowledged that those thoughts would be like telling her: "heal yourself, and then come back." I was able to observe myself and recognize it was I who wished she would sit-in for a whole session, as if "being a good analyst" was measured by her punctual attendance to the sessions.

The counter-transference impact of the patients' absence is something that has been studied little (Urtubey, 1995). From the transference viewpoint, it has been assumed to be a sort of equation in which "absence equals resistance." I will not dwell on this fact here or on its possible meanings, but it might be important to study them in more depth.

Soaked with these types of interpretations, I searched to give her absence a new meaning. At first, the 1975 article by Green, "Analyst, Symbolization and an Absence of Framing," was of great help. I wondered: What would transform a repeated absence into an almost permanent presence? Was the reference to absence a reference to non-existence, a hole?

Elsa defined her life as flat: she felt she did not exist. I wondered if this "gap" in the session could be a staging of what she felt as "the only real thing" (Green, 1997, p. 251). Even though any of those hypotheses could have been possible, they were producing no movement. My mind had obtained a false, but effective, sensation of safety by adopting the "theoretical" factor. But nevertheless, I went back to *Attention and Interpretation* (Bion, 1970), in which he starts his introduction with a powerful accusation against rational thinking: "Reason is a slave to emotions, and it only exists to rationalize the emotional experience" (p. 1). It was difficult for me to stick to his technical proposal: *"The psychoanalyst should aim to have a clear state of mind so that, at every session, he feels he has not seen the patient before. If he feels he has, he is treating the wrong patient"* (1967, p. 273).

Kant (quoted by Bion) asserted that "concepts without intuition are empty, and intuitions without concepts are blind." The problem lied in how to express emotional matters in rational terms. Where should one stand so that both, concept and intuition, can achieve a transformative effect?

Bergstein (2017) approached an answer when he wrote: "The silent and elusive movement of the emotional experience is transformed into words when it crosses an invisible edge, beyond which thoughts and speech meet."

Through the work of *alpha sleep* (Bion), visual images are remembered in the shape of ideograms. And so, a story started to appear in my head, like a first step. It was Julio Cortazar's *La Casa Tomada*[1] (the House Taken Over) that came to me. I started to see a scenario with Elsa and her brother, listening to a narrative that was telling me that "strange things" were happening. It seemed to me that this fragment could be alluding to aspects that were "buried/retracted to one or several rooms within Elsa's inner world."

I tried to be in a mental state that would heighten my observation capacities to the fullest in the "here and now" of the session; the capacity to be in the middle of uncertainty, of mystery and of doubt, something that Keats (1958) called "negative capacity," helped me listen.

Sometimes, I got the impression that the work we conducted seemed very artificial. We could be talking about the very difficult relationship she had had with her mother, or how difficult it was for her to express her sexual and/or aggressive desires, but the affective dimension of the communication was missing. It seemed to me as if she was killing time with conventionally acceptable interpretations. Bion's affirmation that "the psychic qualities psychoanalysis deals with are not perceived by the senses" (p. 28) sounded truer during those moments than ever.

What I felt most repeatedly was helplessness when feeling such a "frozen" Elsa. It reminded me of the Disney movie *Frozen* whose main character, also called Elsa, was arrogant, vain and would "freeze" people who were willing to approach her. This woman seemed to be condemned to blanket herself in an unending winter because, for some unknown reason, the possibility of accessing spring was denied to her.

It became a sort of ritual to begin the sessions with the statement: "I don't know what to say, my mind goes blank, and I do not know if this can help." In spite of her efforts, it was difficult for her to maintain a receptive attitude to benefit and be fertilized by this experience. I told her that it looked as if she had given up on creating a new life for herself.

After some time and every once in a while, Elsa would emerge from her slumber, and I could hold her in my mind and understand her better. Gradually, she recovered memories of significant losses during her childhood, like her maternal grandmother, whom she had regarded as the warmest person in her environment. She died when she was only 4 years old. She still kept a doll that granny had gifted her, and who was called "*Elsita*" (little Elsa, in Spanish). "I don't remember loving anyone as much as I loved her. Nobody told me about her passing. I only remember a day when she 'disappeared,' but I never asked about her either," she recounted, as she cried for the first time.

Remaining silent during therapy was something that terrified her, because silence condensed an intense persecutory feeling. At some point, she proposed having all three weekly sessions at once, since she had the fantasy that if we agglutinated them, we would avoid the awkward silences. We would be able to discuss several matters without pausing, which was a paradox: the manifested request apparently made no sense, but at a different functioning level, it expressed a desire to be merged, and not to experience silence, pause, space, caesura, etc. At a deeper level, it showed a representation failure.

What I was able to understand is what W. Bion had spoken of:

> The inability to tolerate frustration (silence) can obstruct the development of thoughts. It can tip the balance towards evasion and thus, the development of a thinking apparatus is disturbed. The final result is that all thoughts are treated as if they were indistinguishable from the internal bad objects.
>
> (Bion, 1959, p. 112)

The absence of the breast (*no-thing*) was translated into a series of emotions that, in the long run, would create the existence of the "bad breast," a psychic entity that opposed the presence of the breast that satisfies. An apparatus that would try to release the accumulation of beta elements from the mind was frequently found.

Elsa would also evade reality by means of destructive attacks. She would strike against all the functions of the Self, as memory and attention. Frequently, the effects of the excision were so large that any attempt to construct bridges of meaning would seem sterile or infertile.

But to the extent in which we worked through those difficulties we would gain back territory for the *thinking* that had been subtracted by the *acting out*. Elsa was beginning to "thaw," and she was beginning to recognize signs of steering into an emotional universe. After three years of psychoanalysis, she filed for divorce, she requested to increase her frequency from three sessions a week to four, and she accepted the use of the couch. She changed her physical appearance and started dressing in a more youthful way.

Aside from saying, "*I wish to speak, but my mind goes blank*"; she would add, "*it's as if I were somewhere else.*" The nothingness and the meaninglessness would initially appear with the objective of escaping the painful experience. But later, they were transformed into a "live" external hell, constructed with elements of the "nothingness," insufferable but painfully bearable.

Soon after that, a memory emerged. She was 6 or 7 years old, and her parents had a very intense social life. They would frequently go to parties or other gatherings. She would stay home with her brother, but as soon as they left, she would run and hide in her bedroom. She did not remember why she did it, or what he did. She only remembered that it happened for a long time, and she never told her parents about it.

On a Monday morning after the third year of analysis, Elsa surprised me by coming in early and *saying:* "it's strange to be on time (we smiled). I think that if I get here on time, you will realize that I need you. I'd rather be late, so that you won't notice." I was shocked by observing Elsa's fragility and terror towards the transference intimacy. She was able to "confess" that occasionally, she would be punctual, but would wait inside her car, so that I would not think that she needed me.

In Bion's own words:

> Dependence and being alone are unpleasant mental states. Even a baby seems to be aware of when he/she is alone and is depending on something outside that is not him/herself. Early awareness of these feelings is related to vulnerability and cruelty.
>
> (CWB XIV, p. 164)

The echoes of pain resonated in my emotional state. I started to attune to this split-off part of Elsa by means of the figurability process (Botella, 2003). I once again was faced with the images of a paralyzed girl, hidden in a corner, inside that "house taken over." I maintained these images like supportive tissue, and an analytical space, where one could experience, feel and visualize a sensation of death (trauma), started to emerge. The mind of the analyst, to whom Bion devotes all the text of *Attention and Interpretation,* was transformed into what Ferro (2014) calls "a precious and very delicate lab that needs continuous maintenance."

At the beginning of the fourth year, the desire to suspend the analysis reappeared (it was a recurring theme). During the first session of the week, she described a dream: "I dreamt that you would come home, and I told them not to let you in. But when I went downstairs and into the dining room, I realized you were inside."

The dream associations showed the fear and mistrust of the transference bond. She said that frequently, without truly understanding why, she felt I was a persecutory and very threatening being. Elsa insisted that she had nothing "inside," and that it would be better to stop the analysis. Over and over, I invited her to rethink the decision to quit; and she would always stay. However, in the form of an association, she "confessed" that she felt I was deeply inside of her, and that caused an anguish that would not let her sleep. I used that dream to connect it to her memory of being locked in a room of the house, when her parents were not around. I mentioned that maybe, a part of her kept on being inside a jail, and just as in prison life, she lived within severe limitations. With an agonizing *Eros*, it was impossible to rescue the fragrant aroma of love and pain, because by trying to avoid pain, the possibility of experiencing the pleasure of *being*, nourished by experience, was also cancelled.

What finally triggered change was not the oneiric experience, but the long process that had enabled a mind that could dream that dream. As Ferro explains (2006), it had also allowed a sustained monitoring of the analytic field. It demonstrated that the constant interaction of the projective identification and the reverie becomes one of the essential functions upon which the analysis depends.

Trusting the evocative component of an ideogram (Bion, 1959), I asked her if she knew Cortazar's *La Casa Tomada*. Her eyes went wide open and her skin turned very pale, as if she had seen a ghost. Then, she answered: "Yes, I read it many years ago, and I could not sleep afterwards for weeks. It was then that I started taking anti-depressants. Ever since, Rivotril (an anxiolytic drug) has been with me everywhere I go." This reaction meant that, as in any transformation of "O," Elsa no longer just knew (K) about her reality. She started to really *experience* it (O).

Elsa shared with me how guilty she felt because her brother had had a history of chronic diseases and eventually, she was able to expand on the matter. She commented on how she did not want to be present when her brother died. She did not understand the "before" and "after" of the relationship, because they had been raised as "twins." But when she was 12 years old (he was 18), they parted ways and never spoke to one another again. He started a long journey of drug abuse, and she "erased" him (froze him?) from her life. She remembered that her mother had stopped smiling when he died. "My mother froze me out when my brother died, as she did my father," she said, while crying.

The next session, she questioned why she had never been able to denounce the terror she felt towards her brother. For many years, she had not been able to talk about him. After these accounts, she would go blank, as if she were in a "trance." I suggested that maybe, she needed me to bring her back to life through my questions in the sessions; as if my words were a sort of mouth-to-mouth resuscitation, something that could either be experienced as oxygen to breathe, or something smothering. Elsa started crying. My observation, coming from "O" and not "K," was well received. I told her that perhaps, she needed that I "carry" the necessity of the analysis, that it seemed as though she needed me to convince her that life (the analysis) was worth living. Elsa remained quiet for several minutes. For several weeks, the language she used to communicate was tears. We had rescued the vestiges of trauma, but the dream had made it *real*. We were able to experience "*at-one-ment*" (Bion, 1970). A shift from contents to containers or psychic functions had taken place and, consequently she moved from the past of infantile neurosis towards what is being newly lived and constructed in the "here and now," in the analytical encounter. As Mawson puts it (2011), the psychoanalytic objective was not only promoting insight (K), but also fostering change, when it became *real*.

This fragment also shows how Elsa had placed the fragile remnant of her feelings of life and hope in me. Now, we had to face her tolerance to pain and helplessness.

In another session, I added that maybe a part of her remained in that room where she would hide from her brother. We would have to be patient, so that she could recover that "piece" of herself, the one that would express – through her twenty minutes of tardiness – the message of "I was hiding and got lost. Please, find me." She answered by saying: "Every time I arrive late, I think you will send me away. It is difficult for me to conceive that somebody could actually wait for me."

This continuous interaction is what led to the formation of the container, and to the development of the content. But container and content are not static entities, since they define, create and transform one another. The expansion of thinking is greater the more cooperation there is between both movements.

Memory and perception were no longer excluded. Elsa recovered the ability to give life to her remembrances, and she made of them an instrument to get in touch with herself. Thus, she placed the foundations for her new home, a new destiny. She started a process of being fully committed to herself, was able to achieve a "reasonable divorce," started academic work, and devoted herself to her role as a mother without excessive fear. Growth is not a destination nor is it a goal. It is a continuum that includes the long process of conjugation and dispersion. We change from one mental state to another because it is precisely in the caesuras (Trachtenberg, 2014) where catastrophic change takes place (Bion, 1967).

We were able to relive some of her childhood fears and with that, the complex tangle of needs and annihilation that she carried inside of her. What was more prevalent was the memory of her never being able to stick to an activity with consistency, since she would start activities and then give up on them. It seemed that no one ever told her "*you cannot leave; I care about you staying around.*" Covered in tears, she said she felt I had done precisely that throughout the years and that, for the very first time, she felt that somebody was willing to commit to her. Hence the need for the presence of the object (the real breast) wrote Bion (1962), "*because being in sight is the same as being in the mind's eye, and both are the same as being in the mouth*" (p. 87). This realization made it possible for Elsa to incorporate the good breast through breastfeeding and breathing, through touching and listening.

It took me some time to understand the play of words around *nothing, no-thing* and *thing*. In a personal conversation with James Oglivie (2020), he suggested this triad was related to Elsa's persecuting feelings within her. To express it in Bion's words:

> The patient feels the pain of an absence of fulfillment of his/her desires. The absent fulfillment feels like a "no-thing." The emotion aroused by the "no-thing" is felt as indistinguishable from the "nothing." The emotion is replaced by a "no-emotion." In practice, this can mean no feeling at all, or an emotion, such as rage, which is a column 2 emotion, that is, an emotion of which the fundamental function is denial of another emotion.
>
> (CWB VI, p. 236–237)

Elsa had tried to disappear aspects of herself to be able to bear "existing." Understanding, through the tolerance of an infinite sense, made this assumption possible.

Closing thoughts

In this writing, I presented Elsa's story, that of a woman showing how difficult and painful it was for her to tolerate the emotional storms that emerged when she got in touch with herself and others. She depicted it in very lively strokes. She showed us that the true exercise of an analytical function is not only found in both related objects (container-content); the true challenge lies in keeping one inside another.

When she was a child, Elsa had felt that "nothing" was alive – emotionally speaking – so she started acting as a "thing." She never truly recovered from that. That series of events seemed to have defeated many other emotions, leaving her with only a sense of nothingness as a way to defend herself from more vulnerable feelings.

Through this very long process, interwoven with other paradoxical events, it was intuition that helped me "see, touch, smell and listen to" Elsa. It was how we were able to recover the elements of passion (L, H, K) that evolve during a complex emotional experience. The house was no longer "taken over." She had worked to transform herself into an architect and life-project designer. She increasingly became capable of questioning, a true breakthrough. The seed of hope to rethink herself under a different light had been sowed.

The emotional experience with Elsa showed me the seductive and danger-ous face of omnipotence. The possibility of arrogance taught me that it was not enough to "know" (K) about Elsa's pain, but transforming "O" required *being* the pain (Santamaría, 2014). In Bion's words: "The Mystic does not search all things mystical. He wraps his mind around his/her surroundings, and then becomes it" (1970).

I have proposed that working from a mystical state implied experiencing the ineffable reality, to actively go after the terrors, difficulties and beauties that are part of any session (at-one-ment). It is this state which made room to cultivate the conditions upon which new ideas and wild thoughts could blossom and grow (Santamaría, 2018).

In our practice, we are constantly immersed in a continuous flow of what Bion (1977) compared to the mystical Alpheus River (Vermote, 2017). The flow is moving in different directions, with turbulence and catastrophic change. As with any other type of growth, we cannot capture it through understanding, but we can let ourselves experience it from a mystic mental state that can approach the infinite. It means that we should only *allow* O *finding K*. One cannot try to make it happen, but rather just *allow it to happen*.

Botella and Botella (2000) described the analyst's need to perform a "work of figurability" for patients whose memory footprints are "amnesic." In his opinion, the inversion of the psychic order, resulting from a thinking regredience, can take the mystic to the traumatic event of the non-representation. What I am highlight-ing here is that the interpretations, supported by the images (figures) evoked, were the elements that achieved extending the representation capacity. The delibera-tions by Symington (1983), about the freedom of the analyst to think, represented important contributions to understand that intuition is fleeting. It is a transitory spark that constructs fate.

To quote Bianchedi (2005): "*Bion's theory and method make a model-based abstraction of what we analysts live in our practice around mystical experiences; but they do not transform psychoanalysis into a mystical model.*" (p. 20). Thus,

I concur with Tauzsik (2011) when he says that a Mystic deal with an existence in which ethics, aesthetics, eroticism and spirituality take place in a mutual intertwining (p. 21).

I hope I was able to show that what is required from the analyst to make contact with the "psychoanalytic objects" is to be capable of staying in mental intuitive states. Triggering "psychic movement" (Bergstein, 2018) through this state places the mystical experience at the heart of the psychoanalytic practice. It offers a multidimensional glance, and it makes it possible for the patient to receive the encounter of the session, so that he/she moves towards the observation of their psychic reality, towards that infinite circle (O).

As the platonic expression goes: "God takes hold of the mind of poets, so that they can better express their own" (Hamilton and Cain, 1961). To conclude, I share as a caesura (Bion, 1962), a quote by T.S. Eliot that to me explains the mystical mental state that is required to tolerate the pain of the unfathomable emotional experience:

> But the faith and the love and the hope are all in the waiting.
> Wait without thought, for you are not ready for thought:
> So the darkness shall be light, and the stillness the dancing.
> T.S. Eliot ("East Coker," *Four quartets*, 1943)

Note

1 *Casa Tomada* is a short story by Argentinian writer Julio Cortázar published in 1947. It tells the story of two siblings who have never been married and have always been together in a house; they have dedicated their lives to maintain and care for it. Both are characterized by not evolving in character throughout the piece. After a detailed description of the house we find the knot: due to strange imprecise noises (whispers, the overturning of a chair . . .), these two siblings have to leave parts of the house that are taken over by the intruders (the murmurs). Their incursions end up taking over the entire house and the siblings have to leave, throwing the key down the sewer.

References

Alisobhani, A., and Corstorphine, G.J. (2019). *Explorations in Bion's "O"*. London: Routledge.

Bergstein, A. (2017). The Ineffable. Emotional Truth Beyond Language. In G. Civitarese (Ed.), *Bion and Contemporary Psychoanalysis: Reading A Memoir of the Future*. London: Routledge

Bergstein, A. (2018). *Bion and Meltzer's Expeditions into Unmapped Mental Life: Beyond the Spectrum in Psychoanalysis*, Routledge.

Bion, W.R. (1959). *Voviendo a Pensar*. Mexico: Horme.

Bion, W.R. (1962). *Aprendiendo de la Experiencia*. Buenos Aires: Paidós.

Bion, W.R. (1965). La Cesura. *En La Tabla y la Cesura*. Madrid: Promolibro.

Bion, W.R. (1967). Notes on Memory and Desire. *Psychoanalytic Forum*, 11(3): 271–280 (reprinted in *Melanie Klein Today Vol. 2 Mainly Practice: 17–21 (Ed.) E. Bott Spillius*. London: Routledge, 1988).

Bion, W.R. (1970). Attention and Interpretation. *C.W.*, New York: Basic Books, 2017.

Bion, W.R. (1977). *The Italian Seminars*. Karnac Books.

Bion, W.R. (1992). Memorias del Futuro. Julian Yebes, S.A.

Blass, R. (2012). Sobre el valor del "último Bion" en la teoría y la práctica analítica. *Libro Anual de Psicoanálisis*; n. 27: pp. 87–92, 2012.

Blass, R.B. (2010). Sobre el valor del "último Bion" en la teoría y la práctica analítica. *Libro Anual de Psicoanálisis*, n. 27: 87–92.

Bleandonu, G. (1994). *Wilfred Bion: His Life and Works 1987–1979*. London: Free Association Books.

Botella and Botella (2000) - C. & S. Botella (2003). *La figurabilidad psíquica.* Ed. Amorrortu described.

Botella and Botella (2000) - C. & S. Botella (2003). *La figurabilidad psíquica.* Ed. Amorrortu.

Cortazar, J. *La Casa Tomada*.

Eigen, M. (2012). *Psychoanalisis and Kabbalah*. London: Karnac.

Ferro, A. (2006). Clinical Implications of Bion's Thought. *The International Journal of Psychoanalysis*, 87(4): 989–1003.

Freud, S. (1930). *El Malestar en la Cultura*. Buenos Aires: Amorrortu, 1986.

Freud, S. 1938b/1941, p. 302. Conclusiones, ideas, problemas (1941 [1938]). Tomo XXIII. Amorrortu.

Freud, S., and Andreas-Salome, L. (1983). *Letters*. Ed. by E. Pfeiffer. New York and London: Norton. p. 43. (1992).

Goldiuk, H. (2018). *Trabajo presentado en el 50 Congreso Internacional de Psicoanálisis (IPA)*. Buenos Aires: Argentina.

Green, A. (2011). El analista, la simbolización y la ausencia en el encuadre analítico Sobre los cambios en la práctica y la experiencia analítica. *Revista de Psicoanalisis de la Asociacion Psicoabalitica Madrid*, 63(11): 27–66.

Grotstein, J. (2007b). Bion, the Mathematician, the Mystic, the Psychoanalyst. En James S. Grotstein (Ed.), *A Beam of Intense Darkness: Wilfred Bion's Legacy to Psychoanlaysis*. London: Karnac, pp. 102–109.

Hamilton and Cain, 1961. *Plato: the collected dialogues*. Princeton: New Jersey: Princeton University Press.

Keats (1817/1931). Letter to George and Thomas Keats, in M.B. Forman (Ed.), *The letters of John Keats*, London: Oxford University Press.

Levine, (2016). Is the concept of O necessary for psychoanalysis? Ed. H.B. Levine and G. Civitarese (Eds.), *The W. Bion Tradition*. London: Karnac.

Mawson, C. (2011). *Bion Today*. New York: Routledge.

Santamaría, J. (2018). "Dreams, Transofrmations and Hope" In: (2019). *Explorations in Bion's 'o': Everything We Know Nothing about*" A.K. Alisobhani , G.J. Corstorphine. Routledge, 2019.

Tabak de Bianchedi, E. (2005). ¿El Bion de Quién ? ¿Quién es Bion? En *Revista chilena de psicoanálisis*. Vol. 24 (1), 19–23. Chile: Asociación psicoanalítica de Chile.

Tauzsik, J.M. (2010). Mística, clínica e individuación. *Revista de Psicoanálisis, Buenos Aires, OCAL*, n. 11, pp. 127–147, 2012.

Urtubey, L. (1995). Efectos contratransferenciales de la ausencia. In *Libro Anual de Psicoanálisis*. Vol. XI. San Pablo, Brasil: Edit Escuta Ltda.

Vermote, R. (2010). Reading Bion: A Chronological Exploration of Bion's Writings. In O. Birksted-Breen (Ed.), *The New Library of Psychoanalisis Teaching Series*. London: Routledge.

Vermote, R. (2012). Sobre el valor del último Bion en la teoría y la práctica analítica. En *Libro Anual de Psicoanálisis*, XXVII.

Vermote, R. (2017). On Bion's Text "Emotional Turbulence": A Focus on Experience and the Unknown. En H.B. Levine (Ed.), *The W.R. Bion Tradition*.

Chapter 9

Continuing to disturb the sleep of the world

Bion's intuitions on dreaming and reverie

Joanne Emmens

Introduction

The focus of this chapter is an exploration of the continuing advances in psychoanalytic treatment with complex psychopathology, along with what feels to be an inevitable corresponding adversary towards the practice of psychoanalysis. Psychoanalysis, from its origins with Freud, has never been short of its critics, and as Freud intuited, this criticism may relate to its tendency to show humanity in an unflattering light so as to disturb our sleep. While this observation may be common to all new branches of science throughout history, I observe that the quality of anxiety and protest that orbits psychoanalytic enquiry has been an integral part of its discovery and essential to its philosophical core.

In the spirit of Bion's assertion that our patients are "our best and most highly qualified collaborators" (Bion, 2005, p. 91), this chapter draws on clinical vignettes from patients with complex presentations that I have experienced as illustrating, confirming and expanding psychoanalytic understanding. I examine the defensive structures that seem to unconsciously work to disrupt our work and our attempts to construct understanding(s) by listening into and attempting to translate these defensive constellations within ourselves and our institutions.

The capacity to dream, have nightmares and feel frightened: two-way traffic

The metaphor of 'two-way traffic' was spoken by Bion in his playful suggestion that rather than writing a book on 'the interpretation dreams' that one should instead write a book on "The Interpretation of 'Facts'. Translating them into dream language – not just as a perverse exercise, but in order [he said] to get a two-way traffic" (Bion, 1980, p. 28).

In examining the phenomenon of objection towards psychoanalysis and its opposite (a response of appreciation and containment), I observe that both positions seem able to operate simultaneously. The necessary defence to withdraw from and shield ourselves from 'reality' and the epistemological instinct that drives us towards truth seeking, constitute an internal 'tug of war' tension that

DOI: 10.4324/9781003293385-10

exists in us all. Bion (1967) observed that withdrawal from reality is always an illusion – however convincing. Although such a statement may seem self-evident, I find that it is nevertheless orientating as it tributes the strength and conviction that withdrawal states exude and the manner in which its 'illusion' does (in reality) convince us as individuals, groups and societies of its realness – functioning as what Steiner (2011) terms a psychic retreat that offers a pseudo 'protection' at the cost of mental development and expansive thinking. Winnicott wrote that no advances can be made in psychoanalysis without having the nightmare (Winnicott, 1989). I take this to mean that when experience is able to be dreamed ('facts' are then able to be interpreted into dreams) it becomes thinkable, knowable and conscious so that the way out of our 'psychic retreats' towards authentic growth and freedom becomes visible and possible. Yet nightmares do disturb our sleep and attempts are made to avoid them – including in my experience attempts to limit or do away with 'psychoanalysis' that threatens to pave the way for potentially horrendous realities to become known. I argue that an exploration into the phenomena of objection toward psychoanalysis (from us in individuals and in groups), allows us to trace back down the line of responses so as to gain a fuller perspective of the disturbance as a whole – potentially contributing to maintaining the essential flow of two-way traffic from 'fact' to dream – and dream back to 'fact'.

Continuing the legacy of experience and more experience

Wilfred Trotter (a surgeon and an important medical schoolteacher and influence of Wilfred Bion) wrote in 1932 in a paper titled the art and science in medicine:

> The . . . thing to be striven for is intuition. This sounds an impossibility, for who can control that small quiet monitor. But intuition is only inference from experience stored and not actively recalled. For that reason, we should acquire experience and more experience. Do not let us submit, however, to the delusion that experience is made up of the events at which we are present. A broadcasting microphone is present at very numerous events, but it has no experience. An event experienced is an event perceived, digested, and assimilated into the substance of our being, and the ratio between the number of cases seen and the number of cases assimilated is the measure of experience.
>
> (Trotter, 1942, p. 98)

In its early origins (Bion, 1980, p. 28) Freud (1920) was clear that psychoanalysis did not 'invent' its conceptualizations around human phenomenology as these human internal structures have arguably existed since the beginning of human history as is documented in our art, mythology and literature throughout time. What psychoanalysis 'discovered' and is continuously refining could perhaps more accurately be described as a method to investigate unconscious processes that are not accessible through any other method or by observation alone. 'The royal road to the unconscious' is of course metaphorically traversed as a part of being human and psychoanalysis allows us to access these internal communications through working with free association and dream material, enabling us to develop increasingly sophisticated understandings of our relationship to our unconscious in health and pathology. I argue that advances in psychoanalysis are fuelled by our continuing the psychoanalytic conversation and the refinement of our own individual 'small quiet monitors' as well as noticing and attending to the inevitable obstacles that get in the way of our being able to learn from experience. Contemporary psychoanalyst, Stefano Bolognini describes his own relationship with the received heritage of psychoanalysis as that of a descendant sharing common genealogical roots that encourage rather than authorize his research and ongoing development as an analyst. Without idealizing or fetishizing our founders, he pays tribute to the courage of past teachers who were much more than us alone as explorers into the unknown. Bolognini observes that, "Today we are truly no longer alone, if we choose not to be, and if we know how to utilize the presences and the resources of our field" (Bolognini, 2010, p. 24).

He cites a personal communication with Cesare Musatti in which they discuss the plethora of "photocopied articles, books, recovered notes from discussions . . . that become part of the plankton spoke of and through which the analyst nourishes himself, following his rambling needs and inspirations" (Bolognini, 2010, p. 25). In the following paragraphs, I aim to enter into this plankton in order to expand on my own learnings from my patients, colleagues and our common ancestors.

Pandora's box – and the framing of psychoanalysis as the troublemaker

I have observed in my practice frequent reference to the existence of individual metaphorical 'Pandora's boxes' that patients intuit to be best kept sealed up. For example, a patient may say "Well I wouldn't want to be opening up that can of worms". It seems that an infinite variety of Pandora's boxes function as ship stabilizes so that the stormy seas of conflict will not disturb theirs or any of our sleep or make us seasick. The illusion of being able to keep 'unknown' reality under wraps is a necessary ever-present that perhaps in healthy circumstances allows the transitional space (Winnicott, 1971) for alive and curious enquiry and free thinking without us being overwhelmed with terror. However, when this illusion takes on a concrete quality or is disguised as 'real' then fear is diverted from the potential 'too much' content of the 'Pandora's box' (that a patient intuits can and should be sealed) to a form of 'border patrol' that maintains a state of anxious stasis that stunts dreaming capacity (both day-dreaming in the form of reverie and night dreaming) and therefore avenues towards psychic growth and true healing.

In this state of mind, the meaning of distress, conflict and fear is defensively obscured and diverted from its origins – the message is separated from the messenger and even the existence of the Pandora 's Box can be forgotten (obscured from view by the border patrol). From the perspective of my imaginary Pandora box 'border patrol', psychoanalysis as a form of enquiry cannot be registered and instead is viewed as a potential troublemaker – after all at boarders we are asked the questions and not the other way around. I have often been a witness to, 'psychoanalytic thinking' being mistaken or even 'framed' as the 'culprit' responsible for the distress in a system (in a manner that decoys from the actual storm or crisis, real crime, or unknown contents of the box). The task then becomes to eliminate the intrusion of this arrogant upstart 'psychoanalysis'. I have witnessed psychoanalysis being charged with a plethora of crimes such as being coldly 'blank screen', elitist, arrogant, 'Freud' worshiping' and outdated. In my country New Zealand, I have been witness to psychoanalysis being charged as being 'mainstream', 'Eurocentric' and 'imposing itself on our indigenous population in an act of repressive colonization'. In reality, these crimes and arrogances have and do exist and these objections I observe frequently point us usefully in the direction of illuminating these. However in contemporary New Zealand mental health care agencies, psychoanalysis is anything but mainstream (actively excluded from most of our hospital boards in favour of pharmacological intervention, and occasionally short term CBT) and in my many years of working in the area of trauma I have found that psychoanalysis and our indigenous Maori philosophies (that include a rich tradition of metaphor and mythology) when able to join in conversation are highly compatible and have much to offer each other.

Again, I want to return to speculating on the nature of what is being obscured as well as what is unconsciously felt to be at stake if a Pandora box breach was to occur.

What happens when the war can't be won and the importance of waiting until the dust has settled; advances when the nightmare is able to be dreamed.

With patients suffering from severe dissociative disorders, I have observed in my practice the excavation and recovery of metaphorical disaster scenes. My sense of this is that my patients have experienced trauma that is perceived by their psyches as un-survivable and desperate measures had been taken in an attempt to preserve vital information (akin to a metaphorical black box) where the evidence of these traumas are preserved to later be put together only if the circumstances are facilitative of this. I have observed in such patients that access to this internal disaster scene cannot be directed or rushed and is only possible through the psychoanalytic methods of free association and dreaming becoming increasingly discernible over months and sometimes years.

Case example

A patient named Jane who suffered from dissociative identity disorder and chronic suicidality, slowly depicted a landscape which started as a desolate warehouse where she was numb, damp, and frozen. The scene was grey, dim and filled with rubble with the sense that something must have happened (although nothing could quite be thought). Slowly the scene evolved so that she could feel the sensations of damp and cold and start to look around at the rubble. Over time she noticed sores on her legs that she registered as painful and needing of bandaging and then other parts of herself emerged from the rubble. After many months of journeying in this landscape my patient had the epiphany that the scene was in fact a fallen city and that a reconstruction was possible and could now begin one brick at a time. This repair of the fallen city took place over a 6-year psychotherapy and has been accompanied by what she calls a "quiet transformation" that she never could have predicted but which she would never want to be without. "I'm able to keep moving forward now" she tells me and I won't be seduced back to those 'dark lands' again".

These slowly evolving disaster scenes are very different from the repetitive nightmares or flashbacks that also accompany post-traumatic stress disorder (which my patient suffered from less as time went on). They are slow dawning's where the nightmares architecture (damaged foundations, sagging beams) becomes increasingly visible, knowable, and able to be dreamed and so perceived. I believe it is where the Alpha function (what Bion conceives as our thinking apparatus) or our 'small quiet monitor' (Trotter, 1942) undergoes complex repairs. Most importantly it is in the therapy relationship and is witnessed – there is a sense of relief, momentum and coming back to life. These semi-hallucinatory daydreams or reveries are characterized by an inner restraint – they are slow moving and epic almost in the style of a Russian novel. Although they are frequently gritty and grim, they are not dystopian – there is an alive determination that accompanies these journeys that necessarily postpones any philosophical contemplation until safe ground has been reached.

Winnicott (1971), observes that before we can be disillusioned, we need to be able to be 'illusioned'. This is not a developmental given however and requires a good enough facilitating environment either in early infancy and childhood or later in a containing psychotherapy. Brenman (2006) notes the infinite number of reasons for a patient's history to be falsified and stresses that a patient will not be able to arrive at the truth without a supporting object to help them confront what's intolerable. He observes that "Psychoanalysis doesn't answer historical questions. It provides the security to explore them."

Perhaps this process of using illusory functions to reveal a metaphorical internal landscape allows the patient and analyst together to piece together the architecture of their symptoms born from traumatic response to risk revisiting the disaster scene of what had earlier not been psychically survivable – most essentially this time within the security of a containing psychotherapy.

Casting beams of intense darkness

James Grotstein (2007) recalling a supervision with Bion where to illustrate an advantages attitude for conducting psychoanalysis, read from a letter written by Freud: "When conducting an analysis, one must cast a beam of intense darkness so that something which has hitherto been obscured by the glare of the illumination can glitter all the more in the darkness." A patient George gives rich illustration to this observation in the following example. George (aged 70), suffering from severe and debilitating post-traumatic stress disorder, described a dream where he recalled removing a very heavy fence post that was buried deep in the earth (this was a real event from his young adult life). The post was made of a dense native timber and buried in the ground with a mixture of scoria rock and shells to keep it in place. This post was unable to be budged even by a truck and chain as the suction of the earth, and the supporting rubble, produced a kind of valve effect that sucked the log back towards the earth and rendered the post immovable. Eventually he managed to move the post using a crowbar on each side so that slowly wedges of space were formed. In the dream these dark wedges of space were felt to contain both answers and horrifying dread, with my patient intuiting that what it was that he needed to find was at the bottom of the shaft at the bottom point (but that this was an impossibly terrifying prospect). Associating on this dread the image of a pit emerged with the knowledge that parts of people (including himself) were living suspended in the body of the pit and that it was understood that these parts were alive and wishing to meet with him. In a series of waking dreams/reverie, George descended into the pit by lowering a ladder tied by rope, untying it and lowering it further so that ladder length by ladder length he travelled down into the body of the pit. In keeping with 'the beam of intense darkness' George noted that it was important that it was very dark in order to properly intuit (see) the pieces of himself in their adapted habitat (eco-system). In a continuing reverie George descended down into the 'pit' and was hugely surprised to find himself as a *'little chap'* down there. The 'little chap him' was behind a black screen that was semi-transparent (but difficult to see through as there was no light). To his even greater surprise, there were around 30 people also behind the screen, painting the screen independently from each other with differing colours producing a kaleidoscope effect. As they painted the black from the screen seeped through so that they needed to paint endless coats to maintain the illusion of cheerful colour. I asked what he felt about these people, to which he replied that they were obviously managed by the 'disordered part him' (formed out of his PTSD) who was attempting to obscure the trauma and the truth from entering his consciousness. He noted that this had been going for at least 60 years – and that it was time that it stopped! George later made use of the recovery of the 'dark wedge' to depict diagrammatically (see Figures 9.1 and 9.2) the functioning of his own unique post traumatic response. George intuited that a massive trauma in his early childhood (a terrifying sexual assault by an older boy), resulted in a violent 'tearing' or rent in his soul (his sense of himself in relation to the world). The earth side of the wedge (where the post had rested in the earth) depicted the line representing himself prior to the massive destabilizing trauma he suffered. The line along the post (on the other side of the wedge) represented the 'disordered' part of him following his previously un-rememberable trauma. The triangle dark wedge represented the mass of his post traumatic symptoms (or the multitude of ways that he had adapted his mind to screen memories intuited as un-survivable). The point at the

Figure 9.1 From reverie of George depicting his pre-PTSD state of self

Figure 9.2 From reverie of George depicting the functioning of his PTSD

very bottom of the wedge was the 'truth' (the place where his trauma response was born – and where the fabric of his being was abruptly wedged apart – resulting in the pre-trauma self being kept well apart from any knowledge of the traumatic event). Inside the dark wedge (the pit), were PTSD structures that enabled and perpetuated this arrangement. On the inverse side of the wedge (on the other side of the post, not exposed to the surface) was the 'archive' that was full of (as yet) inaccessible information (effectively sealed away behind the rubble of scoria, rock and shell).

George intuited that his work in therapy had allowed him to travel down into this pit, which was dark and terrifying, yet ultimately liberating as it allowed the dissociated parts of him to start integrating by being able to step by step, dismantle the rubble and access the archive, so he could feel a sense of the 'whole of himself' with these parts of him starting to acknowledge each other and work together. In tempo with these dreams, George started to make progress in being able to claim back his knowing of events, his felt sense of 'being in his own time' and his ability to keep hold of what he knew to be real. Most importantly, he reclaimed a sense of joy, enjoyment and appreciation of 'who I actually am'.

On recognizing the gamble and holding open the hope

I have learned through experience that telling a patient that they have survived the horror, before they can know that they have done so, would be akin to counselling a person in the midst of a disaster scene that they need to ignore their senses and think logically about their future finances and retirement plan. My patients' have taught me that I cannot pre-know what is able to be salvaged from any disaster or how a rescue mission may unfold. They have also taught me how essential the element of persistence against the odds is in the process of locating split off parts of selves. I propose that these extended reveries of our patients with severe post-traumatic stress disorder and dissociative disorders can teach us much about our individual Pandora's boxes as they give narrative to the precariousness of human survival in the most extreme circumstances. They also alert us to the reality of that form of casualty that appears to others to have survived yet experiences a kind of 'going through the motions' or 'ghost' existence. George provides a metaphor that depicts the perilous nature of this 'gamble' based on a piece of wisdom he learned from his father on how to go about joining two hives of bees together. George's father kept bees and according to George much admired their culture. In order to join two hives (when a queen has died or the numbers in a hive have dropped too low) the technique is to place a sheet of thick brown paper between the hives. The bees immediately detect a threat and buzz angrily (two 'red alerts' are raised). However, by the time that the bees manage to penetrate the paper (this takes some time due to their small mouths), the bees have become accustomed to each other's sounds and manners and have a sense of being on a joint mission (in penetrating the brown paper to attack the intruders) and reconcile by joining together as one hive. However (as in the case of my patients), there exists the ever-present threat

of a 'breach' that occurs too early or there could be a particularly aggressive culture in a hive so that a deadly battle could be activated. As in all such intrepid
journeys, even when highly prepared, we can't know exactly how things are
going to unfold or if safety can be reached until we arrive there.

Conclusion

> As close as possible to noumena.
>
> (Bion, 1982, p. 8)

I conclude by again giving tribute to the invaluable tradition of psychoanalysis,
whose contributors accompany us in our work and invite expansive reverie and
most importantly provide the containment in our work where we and our patients
are able to have our dreams and nightmares, paving a way towards authentic
knowing. In his autobiographical work, 'The long weekend', about 'knowing'
(and truth), Bion writes of his own understanding of 'truth' in terms of his hope
to "achieve, in part and as a whole, the formulation of phenomena as close as
possible to noumena" (Bion, 1982, p. 8). Central to the psychoanalytic journey
is our attempts as therapists and patients to come into as close proximity as is
bearable to what it is that we are examining. Both Bion and his teacher Trotter
give tribute to the inherent 'tug of war' complexity of this task. Trotter writes
that "the mind likes a strange idea as little as the body likes a strange protein and
resists it with a similar energy" (Trotter, 1941, p. 186). Gaining live proximity to
our individual and group resistances that block and stymie our intuitive capacities for perceiving strange, difficult or even nightmarish reality is an essential
part of understanding the phenomenon of our defences as a whole (analogous
perhaps to observing a planktonic eco-system in the wild). Bion reminds us of
the importance of remaining alert to the tracking of symptoms in both directions.
Tracing symptoms backwards so as to speculate on their origins as well as for-
wards in order to translate their ongoing and evolving manifestations and adapta-
tions. "The problem [Bion reasons] is not a mind with one track, but a track that
is one way" (Bion, 1980, p. 11). The defensive mechanisms that work to build
and maintain a one way track that guards against any retrospective backflow of
thinking are complex operations that require on-going maintenance (in the form
of post traumatic symptoms). The valuable data contained in our patients' reveries that evolve in their own time allow us glimpses into the architecture of these
complex defensive structures in their infinite variety of form. They show how
the mechanisms that allow us to hold back the nightmare are not static defences
but complex organizations that evolve in their destructive sophistication often
silently and outside of our awareness. How grateful and privileged I feel towards
my many patients' who have allowed me to accompany them on their illuminating reveries and to the rich cultural inheritance of psychoanalysis that fosters
and facilitates this invaluable accumulation of 'learning from experience' (Bion,
1962).

References

Bion, W. (1967a). Second thoughts. New York. Jason Aronson.

Bion, W. (1977). Caesura. *Two papers. The Grid and Caesura*. London: Karnac Books. 1989.

Bion, W. (1962). *Leaning from Experience*. London: Karnac Books.

Bion, W. (1980). *Bion in New York and Sao Paulo and Three Tavistock Seminars*. London: The Harris Meltzer Trust.

Bion, W. (1982). *The Long Week-end 1897–1919. Part of a Life*. London: Karnac Books.

Bion, W. (2005). *The Italian Seminars*. London: Karnac Books.

Bolognini, S. (2010). *Secret Passages: The Theory and Technique of Interpsychic Relations*. London: Routledge.

Brenman, E. (2006). *Recovery of the Lost Good Object*. New York: Routledge.

Freud, S. (1920). *Beyond the Pleasure Principle*. The Standard Edition of the Complete Psychological Works of Sigmund Freud. Vol. XVIII.

Grotstein, J. (2007). *A Beam of Intense Darkness*. London: Karnac Books.

Steiner, J. (2011). *Seeing and Being Seen: Emerging from a Psychic Retreat*. London: Routledge.

Trotter, W. (1941). *The Collected Papers of Wilfred Trotter*. Oxford: Oxford University Press.

Winnicott, D. (1971). *Playing and Reality*. New York: Brunner-Routledge.

Winnicott, D. (1989). *Psycho-analytic Explorations*. London: Routledge; Taylor & Francis Group.

Chapter 10

Intuition and texture in reverie

Fulvio Mazzacane

From a Bionian perspective, the alpha function is the basic metapsychological concept that enables us to think of reverie as a technical tool. Reverie is a factor within alpha function and works to transform beta elements, projective identifications, or for that matter, everything that is being experienced as unknown or "too much", keeping the ♀♂ parameter in mind.

Bion (1967, 1992) calls reverie the mental state that is open to the reception of all the objects deriving from the loved object, the mental state of the mother who is able to receive her child's projective identifications, independently of whether they are felt as good or bad.

So, the concept of reverie comes into being in order to explain the vicissitudes of the infant's development within its relationship with the mother, the way in which faith in the transformative possibilities of the relationship is transmitted. It becomes a technical tool for the analyst in post-Bionian developments, in which the emphasis is on the *hic et nunc* of the session and the development of the oneiric as an element of emotional transformation. In my opinion, the evolution of the concept rests on the Bion of the clinical seminars in which, while not theorizing it, he continually shows his capacity for oneiric intuition in working with the clinical material in order to produce what he called "second looks".

Reverie lends itself to describing what Bion means by extension of meaning, myth, and passion: a process which takes its life from a perceptual element which enlarges its scope in the analyst's mind and sets up a comparison with its mythological aspects (the analysand's family and personal myth, the analyst's theoretical myths), deconstructing and amplifying its meaning. The analyst may share some parts of it with the analysand in order to open up new perspectives and find a way of getting closer to the emotional reality of the session.

The first pole of reverie: intuition in Bion

In *Experiences in Groups* (1948) Bion declares his intention to investigate group phenomena through the development of psychoanalytic intuition, a tool which enables him not to depend on preexisting psychoanalytic theories. He wants to

DOI: 10.4324/9781003293385-11

avoid the prejudices and haloes of meaning that accumulate over time and make psychoanalytic concepts lose their revolutionary power.

Intuition (Bion, 1963, 1967, 1970, 1997) gradually becomes the main tool of analytic work, the only way to solve the problem of the mind's inadequacy in grasping the dynamics of mental states. It permits the capture of thoughts which exist before the thinker, the ultimate reality whose existence is independent of the senses and cannot be empirically verified.

In *Transformations*, intuition encounters the concept of O and its differentiation from K. Intuition helps us get into contact with the way the patient's personality manifests itself in the session. Evolutions in O concern experiences of facts or mental states that are still unknown, not communicable but endowed with an intense emotional charge that is released when one comes into contact with indistinct and disorganized elements relating to the analytic couple.

When we start to communicate an intuition, we take into account the restricting nature of representation, but if we avoid the frustration attendant on this restriction, we will not be able to generate alpha elements. Representation requires some derivatives of O and involves features related to K, because when the concept takes form in clinical practice the O-K opposition becomes less rigid.

The second pole of reverie: narrative texture

For Bion (1967), the presence of thought creates the development of the thinking function, like the story we develop in the session, giving form to a note out of tune, to a communicative anomaly, creating a narrative function for that which is devoid of meaning. The analyst's intuition arises from verbal and non-verbal elements, but it is by means of words that the analyst gives form to intuition and starts the processes of thinking.

Some reflections on what I mean by narrative function:

•   Narration is an activity of our mind that has the aim of correlating and interpreting events, finding nexuses of causality, acquiring the awareness of internal changes, and adapting itself to the context. We need to give a meaning to events, especially when we experience changes in which there is a more evident discontinuity. The hypotheses we make when we try to give meaning to events or emotion nevertheless have a narrative structure in a dialogic context (with another person or between parts of ourselves) that fosters the possibility of capturing a range of perspectives.
•   The analytic dialogue activates a continual and reciprocal effort of translation in a constant negotiation of meaning that begins on the semantic level. In lexical choices there is a trace of our defensive moves, of the plurality of our identity, of the legacies and scars that every single experience has produced in the absolutely unique way each human being has lived it. Linguistic nuances are not random but contain elements that reveal the individual's style and psychological profile and relate to the dialogic exchange not only

as an attempt at mutual understanding, but also as a place for reducing emotional distance. The narrative style initially depends on the narrative experiences gifted to us in the early phases of life, becoming over time an original resource, which accompanies us over the course of our growth.

• The narrative approach in psychoanalysis contains a strong ethical option: it is a way for the analyst to be in the session when participating with the patient in building sense in a strongly dialogic way, abandoning the presumption of absolute knowledge and considering his theories and interpretative hypotheses as partial and in a constant state of becoming; to be an analyst who promotes the circulation of thoughts and emotions rather than the linear routes that lead to a conclusive interpretation, who tries to forget theory, having in mind the experimental component that is intrinsic to every analytic journey.

• The narrative game that is initially created in analysis is between certain mythic schemes of reference, personal, familiar, and cultural, which the patient brings, and the way in which these color and obstruct his objectives. By definition, mythic structure has a narrative dimension organized sequentially with a series of linear relationships of cause and effect that are good for repetition, but not so good for highlighting the new. Its musical model is the theme and variations: a strong nucleus from which some possible evolutions take their starting point (Blumenberg, 1979). The analytic field model and narratology have in common the gradual shifting of interest from repetitive elements to differential ones. In the session we increasingly tend to illuminate the original aspects, the place for bringing about the transformations that reverberate in the patient's internal world, in his relational life, in the way in which he may be able to rethink his own history. The novelty of the analytic encounter allows the emergence of new dimensions and obscure parts, renders the material less familiar, fostering an effect of strangeness.

• The qualities of narrative (Bruner, 1991) that are prioritized in the analytic session are: attention to stories that violate the accustomed canons and seem surprising in some way; their role as a container that allows the relational facts to emerge "*in vivo*"; the margin of uncertainty in the way they unfold, which allows potentially infinite rewritings; the opaque relationship between the world created in the session and the real world; the preference for circular rather than linear paths; continual negotiation between differing points of view; belonging to a narrative genre that delineates the emotional background.

A session

Bruna is a young woman, the session I am presenting relates to the start of the second year of analysis, after the summer break, and show a direction opened up by Bruna's words as they passed through reverie and were then played out in the field. The background themes are building up a climate of trust so as to be able to address subjects that are ever more challenging from an emotional viewpoint; the impact of the first summer break on the couple; the search for the right "step" to take without incurring too many risks.

B.   I'm trying to stay calm, to manage the turmoil that takes me over sometimes. You know the skin that hold sausages together?
A.   It is very thin; it works if you don't pull it too hard.

> *[The image of a penis is forming in my hand. I'm thinking that in the dialect of my hometown "sausage" is a colloquialism for the penis, and also thinking about my choice of the verb "work" instead of "hold", as if I were contrasting a gesture of containment with a more "active" verb.]*

B.   *I* have got a problem with paying my taxes, they've gone through the roof because I've earned a bit more. A colleague says I should arrange to be paid in cash, at least partly. I've never been able to do that, but I should. I've started feeling paranoid because we talked about it on the phone and someone might have been listening. It's true, I'm thin-skinned, to stay calm I need to be in complete control.

> *[I try to say something, but she interrupts me, which makes me feel quite impatient. I think Bruna may be keeping something important from me.]*

I must try to talk to my boss about finding a solution. He does everything by the book, but I feel I have got more choice now, I don't have to accept his rules. It's positive to think I've got more work done, but even so I have the feeling that I'm doing too much from an emotional point of view. It's reasonable to feel tired, so much travelling, sometimes I don't know where I am.

. . . . . . *pause*

> *[I think the risk of making Bruna pay her emotional taxes may have made me too cautious. She is in fact robust enough. The image of the penis/sausage is completed in my mind by that of a condom.]*

A.   You were saying that you're calmer today. May I complicate your life a bit? [The condom is still there, I'm asking permission, and my tone is jocular.]
B.   That's what you're paid to do.
A.   I was thinking about the image of the sausage skin, which contains but mustn't be too stressed. What it brought into my mind was a condom, which can work as a contraceptive and as protection against diseases. Where does this image take us? Let's try and think about that. The first thing that comes into my mind is the risk of remaining in a controlling state, being mistrustful even when one has a permanent partner.

[My hypothesis, which I put forward in an unsaturated manner, is that after a year, her level of trust in me is still low. Perhaps I could have waited for the image of the condom to "work" in the field, but I was afraid of losing the chance to make a moment of intense contact develop.]

B.   I had been thinking about a placenta, because today I'm going to visit a friend who's just given birth. . . . It makes me cry, but it's nothing bad. . . . Of course, you want to complicate my life! (She starts to cry.) And don't forget, I've got to go to work after the session.
A.   Let's not exaggerate.

After a long pause, using different words and a different tone of voice, Bruna develops a new version of an episode from her past that she has told me before, a "mythical" story that, by being rewritten, reveals new emotional nuances and the fundamental characteristic of the extreme contiguity between happiness and pain that it seems difficult for her to overcome.

The image of the sausage skin starts up a series of thoughts and shared narratives that speak about the couple's difficulty in finding the right distance for communicating and the fear of creating compromising situations (linked to our mental coupling, the new thoughts that could arise from it). There is something black in the background, something extremely unhappy and dangerous that could make the analytic couple ill. The result of the game we are developing together is the representation of a memory from the past that no longer has the characteristics of a faded photograph but of something alive that contains traces of unsuccessful attempts to digest the traumatic event and the various ways in which many affective experiences in her life have been unable to free themselves of an inevitable double emotional quality of happiness/pain. The important aspect is not so much the memory (that had already been brought to analysis) but the new emotional version that enriches it with references to other relationships in her life and trouble we are having in building up a climate of trust between us.

A possible synthesis: reverie as a process

The analyst experiences various states of mind in the session, from the most exquisitely oneiric to mental states intensely focused on the patient's material; the former oriented towards work on transforming the images, the second more intent on working within the linguistic twists and turns of the dialogue in which an encounter/clash is happening between two encyclopedias, where every word has the potential to start a process of negotiation about the meaning to attribute to it.

Within this spectrum of mental states, reverie is a process that occurs in the analyst's mind, stimulated by the patient's words or by the particular quality of being with her in the session, an exploratory procedure that can lead to the formulation of hypotheses with uncertain outcomes. In order to avoid using words magically, we must also take into account the fact that, sometimes, the exploration can lead us up blind alleys or simply get us lost, feeling lonely or powerless states of mind. As soon as the brackets are closed, the reverie needs to be subjected to translation in order to become useful material, which may be a long job or a short one. We cannot rule out the possibility that sometimes the images may tend to impose themselves and parts of them may be presented to the analysand. Such a situation is obviously not without potential dangers because it tends to have a considerable impact on the analytic couple who are less protected by their respective roles.

Reverie, therefore, is a process that may have various functions and different outcomes:

- An oneiric stroll alongside the patient's text, after which the analyst returns laden with sensations, characters, metaphors, and insights that can be played with in the relationship and thus becomes the cradle of the "third".
- A maintenance operation on the analyst's mind that enables him to pause for a while in an oasis during those moments when the analytic atmosphere is hard to tolerate, and dream possible developments of the relationship.
- Drawing attention to a malfunction of his own mind caused by the particular intensity of the patient's projective phenomena, or to moments when his mind is functioning with reduced efficiency because he is experiencing (or protecting himself against) sterile narcissistic tailspins.
- The unrewarding exploration of paths that may give access to disagreeable feelings that the patient unconsciously wants to experience.
- The possibility of starting to develop countless stories in a clinical co-supervision. Bion's clinical seminars are illuminating about this. They never theorize reverie, or even mention it by name, but show oneiric intuition constantly in action and its ability to be transformed into language.

Reverie's co-constructed quality does not apply only to the initial image or sensation, which is nevertheless impregnated in various ways with the emotions of the two people who are involved in the analytic process. It relates to the work of constructing meaning and is inserted into a way of understanding analytic work that allows the analyst to offer pieces of the image or the feeling that has struck him, so that he can catch contributions in the patient's responses that enable him to expand their meaning or, on the contrary, may act as no-entry signs indicating hypotheses that are irrelevant or cannot be developed at the moment.

Bibliography

Bion, W.R. (1948). *Experiences in Groups*. London: Tavistock.
Bion, W.R. (1962). Learning from Experience. In *Seven Servants*. New York: Jason Aronson.

Bion, W.R. (1963). Elements of Psychoanalysis. In *Seven Servants*. New York: Jason Aronson.

Bion, W.R. (1965). *Transformations*. New York: Jason Aronson.

Bion, W.R. (1967a). *Second Thoughts: Selected Papers on Psychoanalysis*. New York: Jason Aronson.

Bion, W.R. (1970). *Attention and Interpretation*. London: Tavistock.

Bion, W.R. (1992). *Cogitations*. London: Karnac.

Bion, W.R. (1997). *Taming Wild Thoughts*. London: Karnac.

Blumenberg, H. (1979). *Arbeit am Mithos*. Frankfurt am Main: Suhrkamp Verlag.

Bruner, J. (1991). The Narrative Construction of Reality. *Critical Inquiry*, 181: 1–21.

Chapter 11

Intuition

A place for intuition?

Maria Adelaide Lupinacci

Bion was extremely interested in the nature of the bases of analytical activity and of the analyst's work, so he often paid great attention the question of the perception of psychic qualities.

> The physician is dependent on realization of sensuous experience in contrast with the psycho-analyst whose dependence is on experience that is not sensuous. The physician can see, touch, and smell. The realizations with which a psycho-analyst deals cannot be seen or touched; anxiety has no shape or colour, smell or sound. For convenience, I propose to use the term "intuit" as a parallel in the psycho-analyst's domain to the physician's use of "see", "touch", "smell", and "hear".
>
> (Bion, 1970, p. 7)

This is a very clear depiction of the use he makes of the term *intuit* in psychoanalysis. He stressed this term and used it in any possible occasion starting from the 1970s, underlining how psychic reality is different from sensuous reality.

Freud had shown that the unconscious could be captured through its sensuous derivatives, but in this case too, the problem is the connection not apparent in itself between the derivatives from the five senses and what is unconscious and cannot be seen, heard or touched. This connection can only be intuited. Even if sensuous experience is involved (the patient's smell, voice, clothes), what is the mental experience – the transformation of the "sensuous" element into emotion and meaning? In a different way Bion (1987) posed the same problem in his essay "Evidence": what evidence do we have of what we intuit of the patient's state, of what is taking place in the session? With the concept of intuition he seems to suggest the existence of a "sixth sense" for psychic facts. Can we then think of intuition as a perceiving function for mental qualities, as impalpable as the psychic reality of which intuition is a part?

As analysts, we always use intuition, at times knowingly but most often unaware. Micro-intuitions underlie what we usually call "being in touch" with a patient. Macro-intuitions, clearly less frequent, in moments of uncertainty, turbulence or

DOI: 10.4324/9781003293385-12

obscurity sometimes suddenly light up the analyst, and at other times struggle to emerge. However, *intuitions introduce transformations and developments*.

But how and where is intuition generated? With what does the analyst intuit? This question reminds us of another question asked by Bion and his answer: "when the mother loves the infant what does she do it with? Leaving aside the *physical channels of communication* (my italics) my impression is that her love is expressed by reverie" (Bion, 1962, p. 35).

A few years ago, in a seminar I was conducting for the candidates of SPI's Training Institute, a participant asked: and what does a father love with? The candidate was male, obviously. The question was stimulating but I would for the moment leave aside our reflections on this topic to see if they can be useful later on.

On the term *reverie*, Bion adds:

> [I wish to reserve it] only for such content as is suffused with love or hate. Using it in this restricted sense, reverie is that state of mind open to the reception of any "objects" from the loved object and therefore capable of reception of the infant's projective identifications whether they are felt to be good or bad.
>
> (Bion, 1962, p. 36)

Can we imagine a *perceptive organ*, equivalent to the eyes for seeing or the ears for hearing, as a *psychic place* where the intuition of mental qualities and psychic facts is formed, as an "object" imbued with love and hate? On the other hand, the suggestion of a spatial dimension is included in Bion's further expansion of the concept of reverie in *Learning from Experience* (Bion, 1962) connected to the container and to the container-content relationship ($\female\male$). I am clearly not thinking of space in material terms but as a reality of emotional life in the sense that "a feeling of depression" is "the place where the breast or other lost object was" and that "space" is "where depression or some other emotion, used to be" (Bion, 1970, p. 10).

I imagine this *functional space* as a mental disposition typical of the analyst that can be activated in the *specific conditions of the setting in the analytic situation and in the relationship with the patient*, just like in a mother a reverie, the primary maternal preoccupation can emerge at the birth of a baby. I think of this area as the analyst's internal setting. I see it as a mosaic of elements and factors visualizing with my mind's eye the starry sky of the concave ceiling of the Galla Placidia mausoleum in Ravenna: the cobalt blue of the night dotted with stars.

As you can see, I am using a different vertex from the one that considers what should be left out (for example memory and desire) because it obstructs intuition. On the contrary, I ask myself what is needed, what should be there . . . this too is indispensable!

Even if it is difficult to reproduce the emotional atmosphere of a session where psychic facts and their intuition take place, I think we cannot but try to communicate it by describing our clinical experience.

I will present now two rather different analytical situations.

The patient

After many years of four-times-a-week analysis, a pediatrician, a patient I already discussed elsewhere (Lupinacci and Bancheri, 2019), had shown a positive evolution in the structure of his personality and a relevant decline in symptoms. He was more in touch with his own emotions and needs and this positively reflected on his life. But cynical attitudes and narcissistic detachment still erupted occasionally. He treated his little patients with insensitivity, ill-treated their anxious mothers or was ice cold with them; and did the same with his wife. When he re-emerged from these moments he was deeply mortified, but the cycle repeated itself and I had to fight against my own and his hopelessness. After exploring various directions, I was at a loss to find new meaningful ideas. I only tried to keep an internal state of watchfulness. I would like to stress this hard to describe complex situation of total darkness and at the same time of watchfulness, of desperation and dull tiredness and at the same time of waiting. In retrospect I wonder if it was an experience of this kind that Bion had in mind when he wrote that we should direct:

> on this dark spot a shaft of piercing darkness . . . if you want to see a very faint light, the more light you shut out, the better, the bigger the chance of seeing the faint glimmer, if you are not blinded by the light.
>
> (Bion, 2013, pp. 8–9)

Because in the deepest darkness even a faint glimmer becomes more visible.

In a session when the patient was especially mortified and I had more acutely than usual to fight against hopelessness, suddenly in my mind appeared like a flash on a screen the image of the Grid with the horizontal rows representing the uses of thought and in particular *the passage from inquiry to action* (Bion, 1963). I don't know how it happened. Did I allow myself to widen the scope of my thoughts beyond the boundaries of the situation? Was it the force of desperation that gathered and connected data and memories of various kinds scattered in my mind? Was it something in the patient's tone that sounded exactly like this: his difficulty in "acting", in becoming able to enact and realize what he had captured and felt in analysis? All these three things (and maybe others) together? But at that point and in a flash the situation seemed to be clearer: the patient was unable to move from thought to action, actions that represented and realized what he himself had experienced and seen in the analytical situation. There was an obstacle then, I thought! I started using for myself this *intuition* that provided a new view of the situation and this made sense. I conveyed explicitly through my interpretations to the patient the idea that there was an impediment in him, something that obstructed the change he too longed for. The patient immediately took advantage of this. If there was an obstacle, then we could identify it and possibly remove it; it was not an unavoidable "fact". This consideration calmed the patient and mobilized greater vitality and, most of all, moments of intense pleasure in his relationships and his work. His cynical and insensitive attitudes, his detachment appeared more and more rarely but surprisingly it was clear that there was resistance in the transference. The obstacle was showing itself! This resistance concerned a series of thoughts and doubts he had on me as an analyst (and therefore on the value of analysis) that started to become explicit. He felt my authenticity and belief in analytical work and acknowledged that he was benefiting from it, but in a hidden corner of his mind he thought that I was not authentic, that I was corruptible and mundane. Why? It seemed crazy, irritating, almost impossible to accept it for me: a resistance in the countertransference. I was again in the dark.

Then I was struck by the patient's dream of a crazy distressed and embittered person breaking in his consulting room and scaring mothers and children. Was this craziness implying psychic pain? In my mind a connection emerged between our stalemate and an element of his childhood story. An intuition. It was his mother's pain for the heart-breaking death of her drug-addict brother, made worse by the insensitivity of her husband who had treated her as a hysteric and just then conspicuously started an affair with another woman. His mother invoked and evoked affection and compassion, while for her husband hers was just an act. My patient as a child had been traumatized by the ugly violent interactions between his parents that had continued through his adolescence, but he identified with his father in the devaluation of his mother, denying her twofold distress.

> Now, therefore, the pleasure and gratitude deriving from his authentic progress in analysis had to be denied and destroyed, because sensitivity, affect, preoccupation, had to be considered as acts, falsifications of a hysterical mother, of a mock analyst. The authentic investment of his analyst mother in his interest, the distress of the analyst mother for these destructions had to be denied.
>
> (Lupinacci and Bancheri, 2019, p. 539)

Even the patient's libidinal investment of the analyst and the analytical relationship, his pleasure and gratitude had to be denied, as well as everything that could have brought him near to his love and suffering for his devalued and mortified mother and analyst. It was his fear of *feeling pain for the pain of the other* (Lupinacci, 2015) that was the root of the resistance in the transference. In a dramatic session I used my intuition, and I evoked the patient's childhood story and its meaning. This further passage had marked a shift that consolidated in the patient's analysis and life.

Supervision

Reflecting on analytical intuition I happened to see the existence of fruitful intuitive moments in any situation that implies analytical work in a setting that respects and relies on the psychoanalytical method, like in the case of clinical supervisions both of candidates in training or of colleagues who ask for assistance in difficult situations or for honing their capabilities.

In these cases, there are obvious differences with the analytical situation. The basic elements of our method are not directly present in supervision but undoubtedly supervision takes place (or should take place) with modes and in a peculiar atmosphere different from teaching and rather nearer to those old ways of art and craft practice "in the shop" where the personality of the teacher-master, his relationship with the trainee and the latter's sincere passion for the job played a relevant role.

Even if the basic elements of psychoanalytical method are not directly applied in supervision, they are however indirectly present because supervisor and supervisee are emotionally engaged, even if at different degrees, in clinical work and are responsible for the patients. I will mention only a few elements that I consider most relevant in this case. It is "as if" the patient was in the room: transference, countertransference, the unconscious, dreams, the setting are present in the supervision session through delicate nuances of language, the rational understanding and emotional resonance of the analyst who was actually with the patient but is also there with the supervisor. Intense emotional pressure reaches the supervisor through analyst reports and communication. The supervisor needs to activate a specific internal setting capable of welcoming, containing and elaborating what comes from the patient and from the analyst; he must monitor (with a higher level of responsibility) his own countertransference and transference (whether positive or negative is not relevant) both towards the patient and the supervisee. He must also preserve some of the elements that characterize analytical work: neutrality, a regular external setting and along with rational thinking also a free-floating attention to the patient's associations as reported by the analyst's words as well as to the analyst's words.

So, *what evidence do we have* of what we intuit of the psychic state of a patient that is not even physically present and of what happened in a session that we did not even witness? So, I present the narrative of what happened to me in a case of supervision.

A woman analyst is talking to me about a 13-year-old girl who had auditory hallucinations the previous year but had recovered fast enough. Obviously, the analyst and I are still very watchful.

The colleague talks of a difficult moment for this girl. A memory had resurfaced of the anxiety she felt a few years earlier that someone could hurt her mother. This anxiety was connected to the trauma of seeing a rape scene in a movie that somebody had incautiously allowed her to see a few years earlier. The anxiety that until then had been directed to her mother (a sexual woman and therefore a possible object of male desire) now concerns herself and she is aware that it is something new for her, a pre-pubescent girl. She is worried when she walks alone in the street. She tells the analyst that one evening returning home alone she had been very scared. Then entering her building through the garage, she had seen strange bright yellow bands that moved sinuously (and the colleague while talking moves her arms to show me). The girl felt reassured by seeing that light phenomenon. The colleague is terrified in remembering that session because she thought of a hallucination and now expresses her horror for it.

Strangely I am not worried; *intuitively* I see these bright bands as *protective arms that light up in the dark*. But at the same time, rationally, I am surprised of not being worried. The girl's fears and the scary atmosphere had reached me from my colleague's report along with the memory of the auditory hallucinations. So, what is the matter? I know that the analyst has a long experience of difficult cases and in general I trust her. Maybe it is something that has to do with the color and brightness of the bands that does not make me worried? Maybe it is the protective way the patient experienced this event? I am reminded of what Freud wrote in the Schreber case about delusion as a form of reconstruction after a psychotic breakdown: in my mind I see the page of the book. Reconstruction. . . . Maybe what makes me feel safe is what I mentally incorporated of the positive evolution of this girl's mental functioning that we have been following for over a year? Maybe it is the awareness of the intensity that a fantasy can have in adolescence? My thoughts move fast.

With great caution I convey my reassuring impressions to the colleague. She is not convinced at all and is still very alarmed. Then she tells me that once in a session she had evoked the image of a *good dancing fairy* and in front of me she moves her arms in the very same way she moved them when she told me about the bright bands. I am struck by this. And I say immediately with feeling: "Here they are! The reassuring bright yellow bands!" She stops surprised with her arms in mid-air. Now my reassuring prognosis acquires substance and truth for her too. Nothing guarantees that the patient has not hallucinated the analyst's gesture but we both sigh with relief and smile. A *common intuitive evidence* has formed: now we do not need to worry, and time will confirm that there will not be a psychotic relapse.

Something of this patient had come to me through her analyst as if to a "terminal" and activated a mental state, an internal setting, typical of a supervisor, that includes the analyst, her patient, the analytical relationship and the supervision relationship. But its basic conditions are the same: analyst and supervisor work on an analytic object with an analytic disposition.

The scared patient seems to have evoked in a fantasy, unconsciously, with magic intensity, the protective arms of the analyst. During the supervision I thought of Harry Potter and the invocation "Expecto patronum!" that evokes protection against the horrific Dementors (Rowling, 1999). An analyst who can intuitively enter the adolescent world of her patient with a foot in fantasy (the good dancing fairy) and one in reality, keeping a mental functioning between play and reality. Consciously, however, she does not seem to know it and so she is rationally and understandably worried. But something of this unconscious magic game reaches a third level, that is it reaches me as a supervisor who intuitively sees the *rêve éveillé* phenomenon more like a fantasy than a hallucination. The analyst unaware passed to me something of what had happened between her and the patient and that from the patient through her ended up *inside me* in an internal disposition that captures the developmental and transference quality of this experience; a mental place permeated with emotion and imagination, powerfully re-transferred to the analyst by my exclamation ("Here they are! The reassuring bright yellow bands!") that generated an intuitive belief in her.

Further considerations

Let me return to the image of the mosaic of the starry sky in the Galla Placidia mausoleum as a metaphor of the analyst's internal setting, the very place where intuition is generated, in search of some of the elements of the mosaic and of some stars.

Intuition, *intus- ire*. Something happens inside us that brings us to the patients' *intus*, their inside. My impression is that there are different factors and functions well combined and working in concert until not only a meaning, but a state is formed where analyst and patient understand and find each other; where things are evident for both.

In both cases there was, suddenly or slowly, an inflow of feelings, emotions, images, experiences, unrequested memories at the border between consciousness and unconsciousness. *Without memory, but not without memories*. It happened in a psychic condition of receptivity, concavity, always tending to the tolerance of psychic pain (Lupinacci, 2015). The relationship to psychic pain is crucial: to stay with it, to suffer it, not being overwhelmed. In the supervision, I was concerned but not overwhelmed by the analyst's fear and acute preoccupation, probably thanks to my location in a back seat, behind the line of fire, so to say, even if still charged with responsibility.

Along with receptivity what is important is the quality of the emotional links between analyst and patient (or analyst, patient and supervisor), the very source of the quality of the psychic contact. It does not matter that they are L, H or K, provided they are living, true and not negative (-L, -H, -K) or null (no L, no H, no K).These links necessarily permeate also the relationship that an analyst has with his own analytic function. How much do we trust our method? How much love or hate do we bring in our work or how much indifference, routine, compromises? Working *without desire but not without passion*.

In particular, the analyst's capacity to perceive the prevailing emotional quality of the atmosphere of the session, the "key of the session" (Bion, 1962, p. 45; O'Shaughnessy, 1981) is important as well as the quality of his own internal setting, whether it is L, H or K and what sign it has, introducing when necessary movements and inversion of sign.

In the case of the pediatrician, I had to contrast my loss of emotional investment on the patient (what I called "dull tiredness") that led me to a generalized "no" (no L, no H, no K) transmitted by the quality of the underlying hidden negative transference that took the form of the patient's secret belief in the lack of authenticity in my personality. This corresponded to the destruction of the authenticity of his mother's pain and love and of his own love for his mother during his childhood and adolescence (-L, -H, -K).

In the supervision I think that some specific factors played a role such as the structure of supervision work, the good relationship between supervisor and analyst, their mutual trust deprived of compliance and seduction that allowed the flow of emotional resonance favored by a long habit of cooperation not impaired by institutional hierarchy (she was a colleague, not a candidate).

The imaginative capacity, the ability to let oneself be transported by the flow of internal resonance induced by listening to (and seeing) the patient is located at the border between consciousness and the unconscious. When in a good disposition I realize in retrospect that what the patient is telling me and the feeling he induce in me often flow like a film or appear like flashing images. It seems to me that a part of this mosaic is a "dreaming" use of psychoanalytical culture and experience and of culture in general, as I think I have shown with my mention of Freud's work, the view of the Grid, the knowledge of the mental functioning of adolescents and the images from the Harry Potter novels. The personality of the analyst is impor-tant as well as his life experiences and his ability to keep emotionally in contact with them at the service of the patient.

I would like to go back to the reverie and to the question: with what does a mother love? A mother's love is expressed by and through "a mental state open to the reception of the objects coming from the loved object". This means a concave, receptive disposition: one of the creative aspects of femininity (Lupinacci, 2014). A container represented by "♀", the symbol of femininity. Is there a contact, does it have to do with the concave receptive disposition of the functional mental space of the analyst's internal setting? Probably, but not only. For the analyst it is not only a question of receptivity and of feminine qualities.

Let us go back to the father and to the question: with what does a father love? What are the creative, generative elements of masculinity that can become func-tional vehicles of a father's love? I think that today we lack a sufficiently deep and wide reflection on this issue, but we can try to reflect on it and make some suggestions, such as: the movement penetrating reality (the erect penis, the arrow in the male symbol), the courage and strength for being in the world and lead-ing one's child to be in the world emerging from the mother's womb/refuge; the quality of dividing, setting boundaries, differentiating and the courage to oppose a confusing omnipotence; the penis' male quality of linking and by extension its function in the formation of symbols as links between things and their representa-tions and in words as links. How much of these qualities make up a father's love for his baby? For the baby and its mother? How much do we find of these in the analyst's internal setting?

In the case of the supervision, the analyst's protective disposition, her maternal anxiety has been balanced by the supervisor's "let her grow, don't worry, take heart" as a third in front of the couple; in the case of the pediatrician, I think a great role was played by my internal connection to the trust in the analytical method as a protective paternal internal third that supported the analyst/mother discouraged and deprived of resources by the patient's cynicism and destructive violence. An encouragement to remain receptively open and waiting in the dark-ness of uncertainty and not knowing. Open to receiving inspiration from the third represented by the psychoanalytical culture (the flash of Bion Grid) when the psychoanalytical culture works not as a sterile defensive tool to fend off anxiety but as a fruitful element intimately known and assimilated. A feeling that has been represented and interpreted, put into words.

So the psychoanalytical intuition seems like the fruit of an analyst's relationship with his many internal objects that form the elements of the internal setting and of the relationship of these elements among themselves, a creative relationship. The starry sky of the concave roof of the Galla Placidia mausoleum – the analyst's internal setting – seems to be the place where multiple creative couplings take place.

Not by chance, in a different section of *Learning of Experience* Bion (1962) tells that reverie is the expression of the mother's love for her baby *and its father*. This evokes a generative couple. A couple of persons but, by methodological extension, a couple of elements, a couple of factors. Then there is the moment for synthesis: the selected, intuited fact. A generative coupling, or better multiple couplings in the specific analytical situation that is also the place for analyst and patient that contains them, a place that gives the analyst an opportunity to get nearer to the patient's being, the patient's "O". Intuition is an extremely complex experience and does not consist only in being at one with the patient in an inarticulate experience of pure feeling. Intuition is also a representation and to be fruitful it needs also to be a communication. I see intuition as the transformation of what was unconsciously felt/experienced in the experiential moment into something belonging to the area of row B or C of the Grid (alpha element, image/dream/myth), that can be thought, articulated and communicated. A complex unconscious function in the mental space represented by the analyst's internal setting that can cross the contact barrier. Its communication creates an emotional and transformative experience of attunement.

Does intuition create attunement, or does attunement create intuition?

There remains always an element of ungraspable mystery.

Bibliography

Bion, W.R. (1962). *Learning from Experience*. London: William Heinemann Medical Books.

Bion, W.R. (1963). *Elements of Psycho-Analysis*. London: William Heineman Medical Books.

Bion, W.R. (1965). *Transformations*. London: William Heinemann Medical Books.

Bion, W.R. (1967). *Los Angeles Seminars and Supervision*. Ed. J. Aguayo and B. Malin. London and New York: Routledge, 2018.

Bion, W.R. (1970). *Attention and Interpretation*. London: Karnac Books.

Bion, W.R. (1987). Evidence. In F. Bion (Ed.), *Clinical Seminars and four Papers*. Abingdon: Fleetwood Press.

Bion, W.R. (1997b). *Taming Wild Thoughts*.

Lupinacci, M.A. (2014). Female Elements and Functions in Creativity. In L. Tognoli Pasquali and F. Thomson-Salo (Eds.), *Women and Creativity*. London: Karnac Books.

Lupinacci, M.A., and Bancheri, L. (2019). Un caso particolare di impasse e la Griglia di Bion come strumento di lavoro. *Rivista Di* Psicoanalisi, LXV(3): 1–19.

Lupinacci, M.A., Biondo, D., Accetti, L., Galeota, M., and Lucattini, A. (2015). *Il dolore dell'analista*. Roma: Astrolabio.

O'Shaughnessy, E. (1988). W.R. Bion's Theory of Thinking and New Techniques in Child Analysis. In E. Bott Spillius (Ed.), *Melanie Klein Today, Vol. 2: Mainly Practice*. London and New York: Routledge.

Rowling, J.K. (1999). *Harry Potter and the Prisoner of Azkaban*. London: Bloomsbury Publication. Roma, 15.5.2020.

Chapter 12

Infant observation with the Esther Bick method

A privileged experience for the development of intuition

Alicia Beatriz Dorado de Lisondo and Silvia Neborak

Intuition is a valuable form of knowledge. Its etymology derives from the Latin *intuitio*, "image reflected in the mirror". Also, from Latin arises *intuire*, which means to consider, see inwardly or contemplate. We think that intuition occupies a prominent place in analytical receptivity, it is an important part of our operational team (Hahn, 2005; Lisondo, 2002, 2008, 2019; Neborak, 2005). Therefore, we see the availability of the analyst, always in training to a receptivity focused on intuition (ibid.), as a valuable trait that can be developed with Esther Bick Infant Observation Method (Bick, 1964). Why? Intuition often has mysterious ways, even for the person who has an intuition. It seems to us that Esther Bick's infant observation method – with its characteristics of prolonged immersion in the environment where the baby develops – creates a suitable atmosphere for intuition to appear. It usually favors moments of being without memory, without desire, without understanding, with time suspended, in which we are open to the appearance of the phenomenon of intuition. It usually appears suddenly and is often characterized by its lack of coherence with what we have been observing (Durand, 2020).

Esther Bick infant observation method

Esther Bick's baby observation method was created by its author to develop the difficult psychoanalytic identity, always evolving. It consists of observing a baby within her/his family for one hour, once a week, over two years. After each visit, the psychoanalytic observer will write an evocative and as detailed as possible account of the observation, along with the description of her/his own emotional states, the images, reveries and ideas that the observation raised. Once a week the coordinator meets with the group in the discussion seminars and each participant alternately presents the narration of an observation. In the group dynamic, it usually happens that each of the participants tends to identify predominantly with one of the baby's family members, with the baby or with the observer, contributing with other vertices that generate polysemy in our attempts to understand what has been told.

In a family where a baby has just been born there is always great emotional turmoil. The observer has her/his mind as analyzed as possible as to contain

DOI: 10.4324/9781003293385-13

the impact of the experience and of the multiple projective identifications, the conscious and unconscious communications, the silences, the attitudes. All this without being able to offer verbal interpretations and in general neither advice, orientations, nor answers (Neborak et al., 2010). Therefore, this discipline demands the development of a continence to emotions and a negative capacity to be in the midst of "uncertainties, mysteries and doubts, without an irritable search for fact and reason" as John Keats wrote to his brothers at Christmas 1817, many years before the discovery of psychoanalysis! Infant observation with this method also calls for the abandonment of prejudices and preconceived ideas (Lisondo, 2000). For which in our opinion, group discussion is fundamental, where confidence arises in that something will evolve in the emotional contact with the family and that this "something" will occur as observable facts.

The practice of infant observation also helps us for intuitive contact with the preverbal infantile parts of our patients of any age. Those that cannot be remembered in words because they are preconceptual.

> Certain aspects of personality have preserved a primitive mode of functioning closely tied to experiences lived in early childhood; naturally, an adult cannot have a conscious memory of those experiences that have left marks on her/him at a very archaic level. However, if the analyst was able to sufficiently delve into the meaning of the primitive experiences of a baby (and I believe that the observation of infants is an excellent means for this) it is possible to develop a sensibility and a listening of what I have called the "infant parts of the adult patient.
>
> (Sandri, 2008)

Observation in Bion

Just as Freud wrote that he needed to artificially dazzle to concentrate even the weakest flash of light on a very dark situation, Bion (1977) transforms that analogy and considers the importance of "artificial silence" when it is necessary to hear "very faint noises". Darkening in order to see, is analogous to deafening to hear. For Sor (2015) you can achieve "a kind of sensorial alternation, obscure a sense to stimulate another . . . not see to be able to hear, not hear to be able to see". This increases infrasensorial and suprasensorial perception; the electromagnetic wave register is increased. Elizabeth Bianchedi, by placing the passionate psychoanalyst at the center of her psychoanalytic thinking, affirms that

> philosophical mysticism is a doctrine that, while recognizing human reason impotence to solve fundamental metaphysical problems, in order to replace it directs to a special intuitive knowledge . . . many of us think that intuition is one of the instruments of that search. Intuition that at some point will produce a relationship/discovery, through a scientific act of faith.
>
> (Bianchedi, 1998)

Our idea that observation of the development of a baby in her/his family will increase the intuitive capacity of the observer comes from the enormous conceptual contribution of Bion to the transformations that take place within the analytic couple. His book *Transformations: change from learning to growth* is a contribution to meticulous observation. In it he establishes "Transformations theory and its development are not related to the main body of psychoanalytic theory, but to the practice of psychoanalytic *observation*. Psychoanalytic theories, the patient's or analyst's declarations are representations of an emotional experience" (Bion, 1965; emphasis added). And later he tells us that everything that happens in session "can be seen as transformations of an O that is bipolar. One of the O's pole is the exercised intuitive ability". We coincide with and broaden the idea: not only does the clinical practice of psychoanalysis develop the intuitive capacity, but also the observation of infants as preclinical exercise makes a great contribution. At Bion's seminar in Paris, he addresses his colleagues like this: "I am not asking simply what you see with your eyes, but also what does your intuition enable you to see" (Bion, 2018). There, he uses the metaphor of the tree: we see the tree but let us imagine its roots. In the observation of nursing infants, when for example, we contemplate a sleeping baby who was recently born to extrauterine life – perhaps during the whole hour of the observation – there is much that detailed observation provides us, but the trained intuition that allows us to imagine what we do not see based on what we see and hear is essential.

We think that the technical recommendations of Bion, "without memory, without desire and without understanding", will be great allies to achieve a better observation – without the obstructive memory that the past uses as a refuge and thus saturates the field with what is already known. To admit the new and the unknown, the evocative memory that appears without looking for it helps us – without understanding that saturates and prevents seeing beyond that which is known. An example: "Because the baby was born premature, she/he does not nurse well so is losing weight". The premature birth of the baby is an obvious fact, but it is used as an only cause, a single vertex vision. The determinism of the positivist sciences prior to the contributions of quantum physics to scientific epistemology is an example of the same. We think that to the known factor – prematurity – many others can be added, weaving a network of complexities with a place for the mystery of the unknown. We have multiple questions: What does it mean that the baby does not nurse well? We observe how the mother holds the baby while breastfeeding: Is it that the baby does not latch on to the nipple? Maybe she/he sucks a little and gets tired or falls asleep. Did the mother experience "love at first sight"? Is there an enchantment relationship in this mom-baby couple? Do we think that this mother is able to feel breastfeeding as an attractive activity? And, where is the father? How does this couple, the parents, work? Do we have the feeling that the mother feels supported by the father? Was it a desired baby, of the expected sex? And also, why would she/he be prematurely born?

Then we must observe without the predominance of the desire that arises from the instinctual drive and hinders the K-link in the observer. Desire and memory are two sides of the same coin: the baby has to suck so many minutes, has to gain so many grams, has to grow so many centimeters. We then differentiate desire from expectation, hope and faith in the sense of Bion. Nor do we ignore that the exercise of these technical recommendations requires a separate mind (Bianchedi and Sor, 1984) moving through the usual identifications for a working through of disidentification with one's own analysts and supervisors. At the same time, the work of infant observation with the Esther Bick method is arduous, when it is attacked or questioned by some of our colleagues who have not had the experience of doing it. The impact is greater especially when this position is supported by colleagues admired for their ability (Green, Guignard).

Clinical illustration

We will give now an example of the development of intuition simultaneously in the observer and in the mother during the first observations (Neborak et al., 2017).

In the infant observation seminar that one of us coordinates, we listen to the narration made by a sensitive observer. It is the first observation of a baby, Eva, who is 1 month old. The mother, a beautiful young redhead who seems to live with her family of origin, leads the observer to a room where the baby is in a large bed surrounded by her classmates and the family dog. There is a great student-like rejoicing, but the baby seems uncomfortable and cries. The mother turns her gaze to the baby and immediately avoids her, looks at her and repeatedly avoids her. The father of the baby is not present but is not mentioned either. When the observer is about to leave, the music of a sad song that evokes a young woman who must join the convent to be a nun emerges to her spontaneously. In the seminar we decided not to ask about the absent father and wait for Estela, the mother, to mention it. At the same time, we wonder about the song evoked by the observer. Would it be the sign of some sad situation behind the noisy first observation? In the second observation, the mother seems exhausted in her attempts to calm Eva who cries a lot with her eyes open as she stretches her entire little body in the stroller and becomes intensely colored. The observer tells us that it is a cry of honest evacuation. Estela's sister, who tried to help her, gives up and leaves. Estela asks her baby "Evi, what's wrong with you? You are not hungry!" while she rocks her, but Eva keeps crying. Then Estela lifts her gently and puts her facing down over her arm, but Eva continues to cry with the same kind of crying. Suddenly Estela begins to tell the observer, in a calm and evocative voice, that Eva ate at noon and fell asleep, and later they went by car to the bank with Eva sleeping in the baby backpack, and when they returned to the car, she breastfed her. While Estela tells this story, Eva stops crying and before she ends the dialogue, she falls asleep. Estela and the observer remain silent for a few minutes. Then Estela announces that she is going to put her baby to bed, but before that she will change her position so that she will not wake up. With slow, deliberate, and very smooth movements, she moves her from the facing down position over her arm to rest the head on her chest almost at the birth of the neck. The observer describes this movement as rhythmic and very coordinated and recognizes that it produced her an aesthetic impact. As if it were a dance movement and at the same time deeply affectionate. After a few minutes, Estela puts her baby down very gently in the Moses basket. A comfortable silence follows, that Estela interrupts to say that she sees Eva more and more similar to her. "From the eyes down, she looks just like me! Not the eyes, the eyes are similar to those of the dad". That was not only the first mention of the unknown father, which made us imagine that Estela had fallen in love with a man's eyes, it was also an attempt to make Eva familiar, belonging to her family, when the mother found her a resemblance to herself. Then, there were two well-defined moments in this observation. A first moment in which Eva's body made irruption into the scene, Eva cried, screamed, with her whole body; we thought that wanting to evacuate intolerable sensations. There seemed to be no possible continent for that crying that the mother intuitively recognized was not a product of hunger. Until Estela, who seems to be developing a bond of trust with the observer, goes on rocking her baby, now with her words, with which she weaves the quotidian story of the lives of them both. Then the baby is silent, the baby relaxes, the baby falls asleep and now a body-mind harmony appears on the scene, which also constituted a moment of harmony between the three protagonists. What are the links of the psychic birth of the human infant? This one that I describe seems to me to be one of those links (Bion, 1987; Neborak, 2005, 2015).

In the successive observations Estela could tell the observer about Eva's father who disappeared when he found out she was pregnant, and of her decision to have Eva anyway when her parents strongly supported her. Then, the song evoked by the observer in the first observation became important for us, as result of her intuition about Estela's mental state.

The observer's intuition also played a central role in the observation that took place when Eva was 7 months old, in which Estela told her moving story. Eva slept on her grandparents' bed and the observer was not comfortable being alone with the baby in that room while the mother studied in a faraway place. Estela seemed to realize Valeria's (the observer) discomfort and sat on the carpet, very relaxed, to share a time with her while eating a sandwich. The emotional climate was transformed, it became intimate. At that moment, the observer came up with a question that for some time she wanted to ask Estela and allowed herself to formulate it. "Is there anything you would like to tell me? Anything you have thought about Eva?" To which Estela responded quickly: "Yes, sometimes I thought it was important for you to know about Eva's dad". Valeria replied that if she wanted to, she could tell her, and before she was able to finish the sentence, Estela began to tell her. It was a sad story, the father who disappeared, who did not want to know anything about that pregnancy, Estela who doubted having the baby, her parents who had lost a child and held her emotionally to have this baby. The moment Estela tells the observer "I decided to have her and raise her alone", Eva, who was sleeping, opened her eyes widely, waking up, looking around without seeing anything. She didn't look startled, she seemed to be trying to capture sensations with her eyes. When she fixed her gaze she focused on Valeria, who smiled at her, and Eva opened her eyes even bigger. In the group meeting we went through different emotions when we listened to this observation. At first, with Valeria's discomfort facing the fact of being left alone with the baby in the grandparents' room. We thought that the observer seemed to feel that she was "invading someone else's space" (trespassing) feeling troubled to maintain the setting under those circumstances. Estela's attitude when changing plans, made us think that she understood the mood of the observer. But also, that something moved her to approach Valeria as if her need to speak had arisen at that moment, before the moment the observer formulated her question. Estela's immediate response led us to conjecture that there could had been some unconscious-to-unconscious communication between the two of them. It was clear to us that Estela was looking forward telling Valeria her story and that it was important for her to communicate her circumstances. At the same time, we thought that the observer had the question at the tip of her tongue for a while and yet, she asked it at that instant when her intuition indicated that it was the appropriate moment. Bion's words were present to us at that moment: "the psychoanalyst will not only have to develop her/his power to intuit, but will need to keep it in good condition, as an eye surgeon must keep the muscles of his hands in perfect condition" (Bion, 1977).

Conclusion

Bion formulated an observation theory of psychoanalysis. He emphasized the importance for the analyst to intuit the emerging emotions in the bond before they become painfully evident. For him, to avoid unnecessary pain constituted one of the goals of intuition.

"O", psychic reality, is a bipolar concept like so many other Bion's ideas. One pole is the exercised intuitive ability. We can think that the question that was not silenced in Valeria's mind could be asked at the opportune moment because of her exercised intuitive ability in the intimate and prolonged contact with the mother and her baby.

By sharing the baby's life on a weekly basis with her multiple relationships, the observer makes imaginative and rational conjectures in creative ways: they are an invitation to develop her/his ability for intuition. She/he conquers a broader horizon that favors contact with her/his own primitive preverbal mental states. If this contact is tolerated, self-knowledge may become a compass for exploring "the baby parts" of patients.

References

Bianchedi, E.T. (1998). El psicoanalista apasionado o aprendiendo de la experiencia emocional. *Psicoanálisis APdeBA*, XX(3).

Bianchedi, E.T., y Sor, D. (1984). *La mente primordial, el mito de Babel y la mente separada. Actas del V Simposio y Congreso interno de APdeBA sobre "Desarrollo psíquico temprano".*

Bick, E. (1964). Notas sobre la observación de lactantes en la enseñanza del psicoanálisis. *Revista de Psicoanálisis*, XXIV(4).

Bion, W.R. (1965). *Transformations*. London: Karnak Books, 1984. *Transformaciones. Del aprendizaje al crecimiento*. Centro Editor de América Latina, 1972.

Bion, W.R. (1977). Caesura. In *Two Papers, The Grid and the Caesura*. Río de Janeiro: Imago, 1977. Cesura. En La tabla y la cesura. Buenos Aires, Gedísa, 1982.

Bion, W.R. (1987). *Clinical Seminars and Four Papers*. Ed. F. Bion. Abingdon: Fleetwood Press. [Reprinted in *Clinical Seminars and Other Works*. London: Karnac Books, 1994].

Bion, W.R. (2018). *El seminario de Wilfred Bion en París, julio de 1978*. Ed. Biebel, R. López Corvo, y L. Morabito.

Durand, N. (2020). Comunicación Personal.

Hahn, A. (2005). Acerca de la intuición. In *Presentado en la clínica Tavistock en noviembre de 2005*.

Lisondo, A.B.D. (2000). A observação de bebês: o compromisso da psicanálise quando os maus tratos são psíquicos. *Psicanálise em Revista*, 1(1): 81–87.

Lisondo, A.B.D. (2008). Um analista no trabalho Clínico. In *Psicanálise de Bion Transformações e Desdobramentos*. SBPSP.

Lisondo, A.B.D. (2019). A observação psicanalítica: Instrumento privilegiado na construção da identidade analítica. Os vértices de Bick, Bion E Meltzer. In N.R.A.F. França (Ed.), *Observação de bebês: Método e aplicações*. São Paulo: Blucher, pp. 33–62.

Meltzer, D. *The apprehension of beauty*.

Neborak, S. (2005). Del otro lado de la impresionante cesura. *Presentado en el panel de Traumas Prenatales, durante el 44° IPAC en Río de Janeiro*. Brasil, julio de 2005.

Neborak, S. (2015). El cuerpo presencia o intrusión. Notas sobre armonías o disarmonías cuerpo-mente. *Presentado en el 2° simposio de la Sociedad Psicoanalítica de Mendoza*, octubre de 2015.

Neborak, S., Fernandez, V., Apel, V., Biotti, F., Camacho, J., and Oelsner, J. (2017). ¿Quién ejerce la función paterna? *Presentado en el 10° Congreso Internacional de Observación de bebés*. Torino, Italia, noviembre de 2017.

Neborak, S., Weis, M., Fernandez, V., and Reingold, M. (2000). De la mirada "fascinada" a la mirada de "conocimiento" en la observación de un bebé. Transformaciones en el desarrollo de un vínculo. *Presentado en el 5° Congreso Internacional de Observación de la relación madre-bebé*. Río de Janeiro, Brasil, agosto de 2000.

Sandri, R. (2008). L'observation dans la situation analytique. *Presentado en el VIII congreso internacional de observación de lactantes con el método Esther Bick*, Buenos Aires, agosto 2008. (Traducción nuestra).

Sor, D. (2015). Introducción y psicoanálisis. In *Revista de la Asociación Psicoanalítica Colombiana*. Vol. XXVII, N° 2.

Chapter 13

Interpretation and intuition

Transmission of scientific contents and emotional contexts in psychotic fields

Guelfo Margherita, Alexandre Patouillard, Federico Pone, Salvatore Rotondi and Loredana Vecchi

The workshop we refer to in this chapter concerns the experience of noetic and affective movements. It occurred in a space-time occupied by a large group (65 people) that lasted two hours and was held simultaneously with other workshops within an international meeting on Bion's work. The focus here is put both on the need, given or emerging, for the group to process the psychoanalytical theory discussed and exchanged (contents), and on the conscious simultaneous construction of the evolving affective field (context) within a self-conferred (by its own being there) multilevel group identity: in the group as in the meeting, as in Bionian theory.

To favor transformations, the doors were kept open, as boundaries semipermeable to new comings and goings among confusions and questions because of phones ringing, delays, mix-ups of geography, languages, rules, power (who institutes the field while the group is settling in?), strangers, leaderships, establishments, mysticisms; shall we talk in an orderly fashion or follow free associations and free enactments, allowing the field to feel vital while performing its scientific assignment?

We are observing from inside an insane asylum! Like a psychotic field, busy with melting into entropy the information structuring and containing it; a beta field, for the massive prevalence of beta elements among those traversing it; an "O" field, for its malleability in being able to exist toward any evolution the energy structures itself as either collapse or basic assumption.

The working hypothesis: we are observing how within this psychotic field a thought is structuring, without dissolving the field, that can be brought to the formulation of, among others, scientific hypothesis – individuating, therefore the point of observation from which can be perceived the co-presence, separated but deeply correlated, of experiencing the vital emotions of the field (container) and constructing the hypothesis swimming within it (contents). In regard to understanding how communication is structured within and between the two levels, we will be assisted by the clinical material of a case.

We then start to glimpse within the field the separation between what Matte Blanco (1975) calls *the two modalities of being*: asymmetric, of information,

DOI: 10.4324/9781003293385-14

rationality, scientific method and language, of *interpretation*; symmetric, of entropy, irrationality, of oneiric, poetic, psychotic language, of *intuition*.

Interpretation and intuition are indeed the subjects of our meeting.

So our group settled in on two simultaneous psychic states, comparing themselves: a *workshop mental state* in which the group takes back identity and cooperation to construct an emotional context of the "Us" and to better bear the development of collaboration, intuiting, despite everything, the importance of being together as one; a *seminar mental state* that uses group efficacy, in relation to the assignment, as an incentive.

Being divided, separated, as in Shannon's (Shannon & Weaver, 1949) second theorem about channel coding, allows one to transfer more "quanta" of information as they are distributed simultaneously among multiple channels.

Within a seminar about Bion's thought, in a Bionian meeting, it's not necessary to explain the symbols he uses. It will be enough, observing Figure 13.1, to note its flow to the right or left so that the two fields are superposed, simultaneously mixing and staying distinct depending on the viewpoint we assume.

Interpretation is located in the *asymmetric modality*, adopting its logics and languages; *intuition* instead is located in the *symmetric modality* and melts in the oneiric entropy the logics and languages of the infinite sets.

The workshop emerges now from psychotic fields as any "human" aggregate located in any space-time portion whatsoever.

So, a human aggregate is born from the confusions of the "O" field due to the crossing and overlapping of the concentric boundaries between individuals, micro-groups, workshops, our scientific meeting, the city, psychoanalysis, the

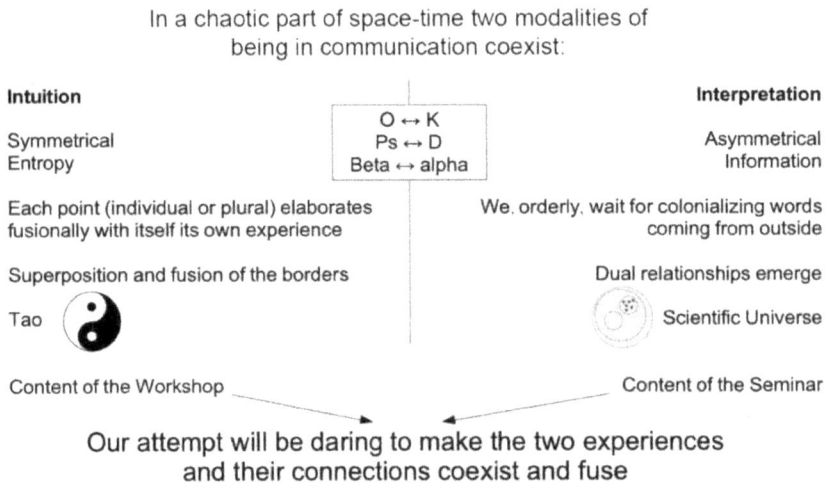

In a chaotic part of space-time two modalities of being in communication coexist:

Intuition		Interpretation
Symmetrical	O ↔ K	Asymmetrical
Entropy	Ps ↔ D	Information
	Beta ↔ alpha	
Each point (individual or plural) elaborates fusionally with itself its own experience		We, orderly, wait for colonializing words coming from outside
Superposition and fusion of the borders		Dual relationships emerge
Tao		Scientific Universe
Content of the Workshop		Content of the Seminar

Our attempt will be daring to make the two experiences
and their connections coexist and fuse

Figure 13.1

Fields, entities and energies

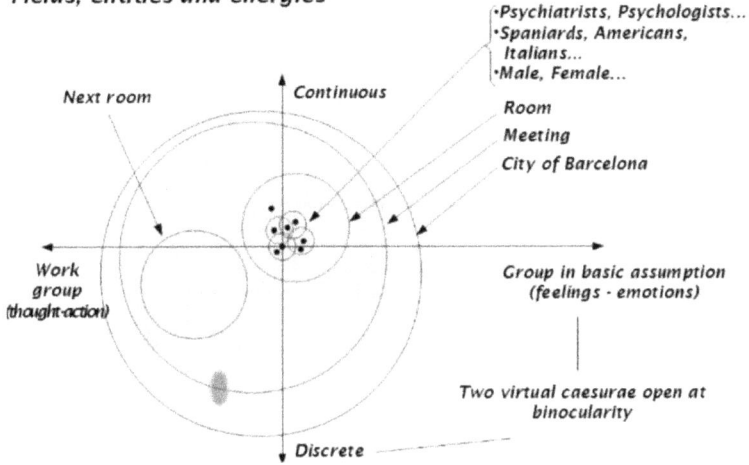

Figure 13.2

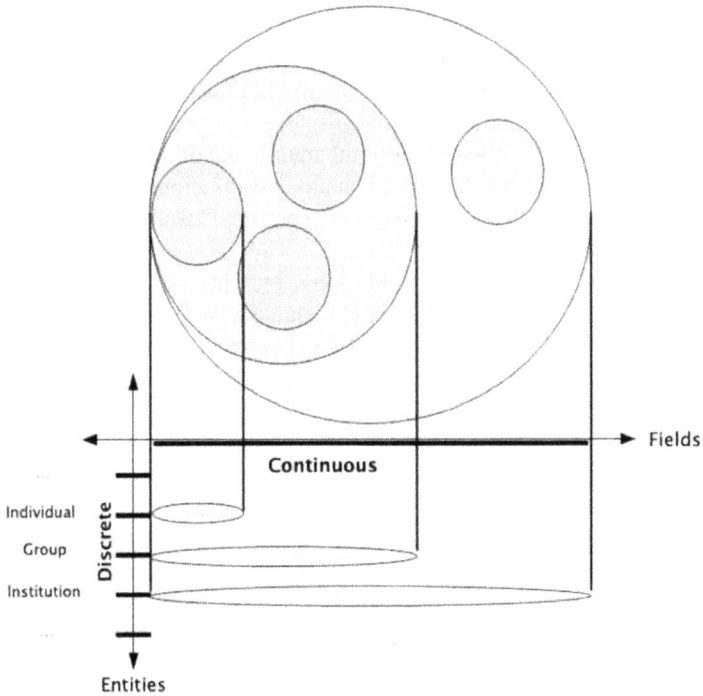

Figure 13.3

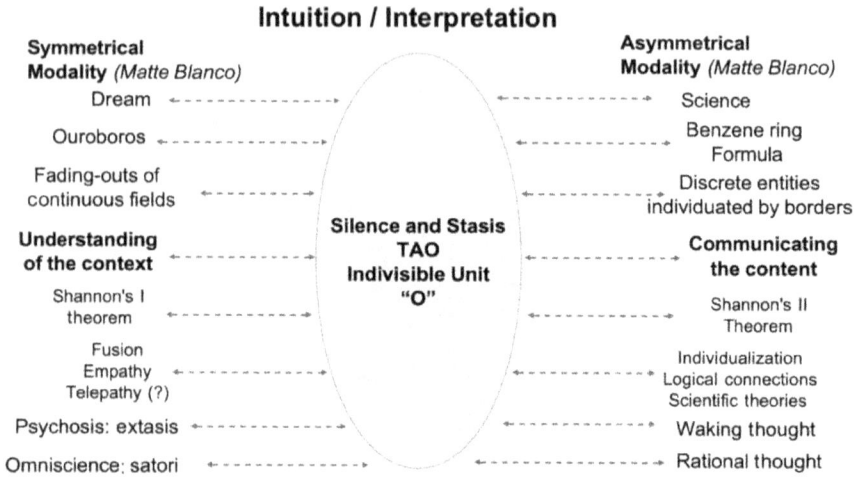

Intuition / Interpretation

Symmetrical Modality *(Matte Blanco)*		Asymmetrical Modality *(Matte Blanco)*
Dream		Science
Ouroboros		Benzene ring Formula
Fading-outs of continuous fields		Discrete entities individuated by borders
Understanding of the context	**Silence and Stasis TAO Indivisible Unit "O"**	**Communicating the content**
Shannon's I theorem		Shannon's II Theorem
Fusion Empathy Telepathy (?)		Individualization Logical connections Scientific theories
Psychosis: extasis		Waking thought
Omniscience: satori		Rational thought

Figure 13.4

psychotic groups we talked about – all traversed by different languages, contexts, subjects and cultures. It all happens in a polycentric, matryoshka-doll-like portion of space-time (physical and mental): the "complex multilayer set" (Margherita, 2012).

The semi-permeability to the milieu of the membrane of these concentric bubbles orients the energy flows regarding them along oscillations between within ↔ without; continuous ↔ discrete, information ↔ entropy, identity concentration ↔ psychotic dissolution.

Us as individuals and our "Us", within these bubbles and these fields, didn't start oriented by specific identity functions; to quote Bion in his roman seminars: "We did not know *Us*". We then tolerated our confusion, within the workshop, waiting for the negative capability to give meaning to the new gestalt about the "who are we?" to make emerge.

To understand the context (the bubble universe in which we're immersed) we have to hypothesize that it unfolds in a continuous (symmetrical) dimension within the membranes identifying the bubbles placed like a matryoshka doll. The internal fields are homogenous, continuous and communicate emotionally with each other by symmetric oneiric-emotional logics: "I feel, therefore I am".

In the spaces external to the membranes (even if concentric), reality (maintained by the superficial tension gradients) flows asymmetrically. Communications traverse an external milieu between the bubbles, with discrete modality, reaching them as separate entities: "I am, therefore I communicate".

An oneiric intuition transforms into a scientific interpretation

The story goes that the German chemist Friedrich August Kekulé von Stradonitz described the benzene ring formula after having dreamed of a snake biting its own tail (ouroboros).

Entering his brain, we might start by describing what's inside the central "egg".

In such an "O" field which, like Bion, we might call the "protomental", the contained matter-energy (physical, biological, psychical and social) is constantly being swallowed in an entropic black hole (-K → O) by the fusing-gravitational attractive force pervading it (which we might call Eros or valency). A non-consciousness losing itself in the infinite of "O" and in the silence and stasis of Matte Blanco's (1975) indivisible unit; so, in Eastern mysticism the Tao of Lao-Tse, Hendricks (1992).

The self-contemplative consciousness, in not producing information able to pass the line of the event horizon (so of producing an observer to activate it), can only be static, not dynamic.

So, this consciousness, traversing the chain on the left of the egg, can narcissistically collapse in the failure to produce a distinct human field; meaning a field strategically relatable with itself and with the context containing it.

Therefore, this consciousness can produce psychosis.

The alternative might be to become lost in the super-system ("I" inside the "We") transforming the (+K → O) of collapse in an ecstatic drowning within a mystic dimension.

Meaning another form of knowledge, satori-like, intuitive, syncretic in the sense that one's own self is lost in the World-self: ecstasy.

And it's pleasant to be shipwrecked in this sea.

– Leopardi (1819)

If we consider the "O" field as a field of unlimited potential, all-encompassing, all-embracing all the way to infinity, we can't help but also consider, as an unpredictable quantum leap, the necessity of its possible dynamic evolution along its opposite trajectory, on the right of the "egg" (O → K).

This causes evolutions from inside the field of, for example, individualization, tools of knowledge, meaning, therapy, identity, culture.

"I" (but naturally "We" as well) am my point of view that builds the world.

The contents of the "O" field thus given direction will try, individually or collectively, to build for themselves their own unitary consciousness, to exist and feel alive and vital. So information escapes the event horizon and switches the entropy through plus or minus sign.

In conclusion, the oscillations of the energy flows between the bubbles and their milieu, along the intuition-interpretation axis, can be O ↔ K; Ps ↔ D; beta elements ↔ alpha ↔ gamma; fusion ↔ individualization; magma ↔ objects;

emotional sharing ↔ clarity and differentiation; intuition ↔ interpretation; synchrony ↔ diachrony; cloud ↔ algorithm; dream ↔ science; group ↔ institution; entropy ↔ information.

Epistemophilia

In a large group, within the described oscillation, we discern an information → entropy movement (if we are moving from the left to the right along the arrow) with a loss of common sense.

The opposite direction will be a movement of entropy → information instead, able to integrate meaning and identity.

The psychoanalyst, in regard to large groups and psychosis, should try to not be paralyzed by the fear of the collapse of usual logical frameworks (psychotic evolution on the left of the arrow), but build instead, through reverie, a web of connections (K), entrusting to it their curiosity and creativity, to dive into the forbidden universe on the left of the arrow.

Prometheus and Adam are confronted with patricide and incest as the taboos of every scientific operation (as can be seen in the myths of knowledge). This is the oneiric-narrative side that the bi-ocular possibility, Bion (1977), should integrate to every trajectory or "parabola/parable" in the scientific journey. In this mystic-oneiric-delusional universe, milieu of the large group's incubations, the productions of the latter can resemble Bion's acts of faith, always at risk of transforming into a betrayal.

The mystic and the establishment

The construction of the workshop space, meaning the inside of the seminar, from the start hinges on the elaboration of the emotional identity relation between mystic and establishment. This conflict seems to incarnate the constituting myth of our group's population, like that of the medicine man and of the tribe chief: "when do we start?"; "who goes first?"; "do we close the door or not?"; "how do we organize the flow of communication orderly?"; "are interruptions allowed?"

The experience of chaos hatches an unlimited potentiality open to free associations and to the language of achievement, a synchronic language of the whole group in unison. The cosmos, within which the chaos is ordered, is then used to find the languages of substitution to tell each other about it scientifically. Interrupting whenever so wished creates then an experience of circularity, not oriented anymore by the hegemonic cultural vector, going from the teacher's desk to the pupils: it's not the teacher's gaze that makes the pupil now; on the contrary it's the desire of the pupil that necessarily "presentifies" the teacher, coagulating him around his word.

This became evident when a group of north-European participants lingered at the door, attracted by the workshop's theme, but disappointed that they didn't understand the Italian that had become the language chosen by the majority of the Latin participants to express themselves.

Pep Esteve: I think we must clarify whether in this experience the establishment is involved as well. I have been assigned by the seminar to preside to the rules of the debate. You, Guelfo, are instead the mystic broadening our perceptions. Only the presence, through the establishment, of the necessary institutionalized translators can allow to collect the version in another language of a psychotic, as you say, experience.

The "strangers" decide to participate in the workshop, having intuited that a possibility of understanding exists.

Guelfo: We simultaneously build tools (in a seminar dimension) to extract a scientific discourse from emotional confusions while we wonder (in a workshop dimension) about the roots of the field that makes exploration possible.

Pep Esteve: Anyway, what is now happening is an approach between intuition and interpretation as you have proposed them. How can we share this reality?

Guelfo: A fusional desire, tied to a feeling of curiosity and interest (wanting to participate), and an impossibility to share if basic cultural mediators (like a language) aren't created, not hegemonic but shared, so that we can, after Babel, build together (understand together). The problem we have is "how do we behave toward minorities?" (*general laughter*)

Let's tackle this . . . in here the English speakers are a minority, but in the wide world . . .

Participant: And how come the minority came in here to disturb our mystic peace? (*general laughter*)

Other Participant: Perhaps I'm the minority as I don't know English enough (so I'm psychotic and can't communicate with them)

Guelfo: You can be a minority in many other fields, but not here and now. There is a hegemony in this field here and now, and besides, those who have hegemony want to abuse it. The mystic is the stranger blocked at the borders waiting for the establishment to provide the correct documents. "Am I part of the Agape or am I excluded from sharing because I'm different and perhaps suspected of terrorism?" These emotions, divided in roles, confront each other within the group's script while we're writing it and at the same time, in parallel, those emotions are performed on the fragmented scenario of our individual inner world. What about outside of us? The incredible, fantastic space-time location of our field can be supposed to be tending toward infinity within the oneiric material of a patient of a

Participant: On the subject of telepathy, I'll mention a patient in Italy who almost never calls me, except to change an appointment, and yet yesterday as I was in our hotel room with my colleagues he called, telling me that right now he's in Barcelona (like me, but he doesn't know that). This surreal thing stunned and disturbed me because he was saying that he woke up at night and couldn't breathe (a symptom he never had before) and was very afraid he would die; what's more a friend of his had something very similar and was hospitalized. Since yesterday he's very afraid, and I too am for him, because he hasn't been able to sleep for three nights.

Guelfo: My point of view is that we are in a layered system: historic space, city, individual physical and mental pathologies – what Jung would call synchronicity. Intuition is located at the boundaries of other space-times into which all the contexts might transform. Fantasy goes to explore the intuition of a future as a possible context of the coronavirus. We have to admit that the coexistence of mystic and establishment is sometimes hard to bear, like that of Sibyl and Einstein. Intuition is the more sensitive communication modality to mobilize silence and omniscience. Breaking them makes it so that, traversing the tapestry of dream, the communication modality can be no other than that of beta bombing and of the transformation of the protomental in mental. So the first ring we find is that of protomental magma, then the transformation in mentalizing, through the alpha function, the dreamed beta elements so they can be told, individuated, separated and thus put in relation with each other. This allows the rational and scientific (not only empathic or telepathic anymore) communication of the oneiric field; but to use this communication we have to wait for this myriad of states to all be traversed, perhaps simultaneously, within this multilayer world.

The John Wayne case!

I'm sometimes called upon to perform supervisions, of teams or clinical cases, in psychiatric departments. The setting I try to organize is that of a room, in which the participants are gathered; the door is open onto the happenings flowing in the meantime through the whole department involving other situations and people that can therefore indirectly, I'd say with osmosis-like semi-permeability, participate to our group events, whenever they deem it opportune. It's like keeping the door open at the boundary between a more or less conscious group and an institutional unconscious. What unfolds is treated within the group like a free association (communicative acting out) of the institution behaving as an extra participant to the group itself. There have been numerous cases of real physical emersion within the circle of hospitalized patients who, like spokespeople, participate, both as individuals and as a discourse, encompassing the entire institution and its history at times dramatic, like actual coryphes. At this point in the Workshop, among other videos regarding other group supervisions in institutional contexts, was projected my tale, to a group of resident psychiatrists, of the experience with a patient who presented himself as "John Wayne". The language used in the following exposition will now differ from the more scientific one of the first part of this text, to include emotional connotations, less formal and more typical of a direct interaction: both with a psychotic, and with a collective context.

I was conducting around ten supervision meetings of about three hours each, in a psychiatric department in the metropolitan area of my city. The department was symptomatically described to me as terrified, paralyzed with fear and motivational detachment because of issues in surveillance and searching of patients, responsibilities of attendants and nurses. The doors had been kept locked as a doctor had almost been shanked.

Everybody, starting from the medical and bureaucratic hierarchies, attested interest in my arrival; during the practice though, the hierarchies would never be present, except for a few minutes at the tail end of a few meetings.

The specific meeting I'm telling of, opens talking about: the physical and emotional absences; the commitment and engrossment in one's own work; the wish to run home and the mutual blaming for the total indifference of everyone toward the needs of others. Nobody suffers at work for the other's pain. The apparent philosophy: you must stay detached from problems to solve them. Nobody, it is said, is working on my problems or takes interest in me. Maybe, thinking it through, I do the same with the others.

Who of us is here today? Who of us is here and who is not? The head of the ward is here, who is a jolly good fellow, the nurses and attendants on duty are here, the doctors are here; some, who are very interested, come here only when there's our meeting even though they should be working elsewhere. The discussion opening up is "but after all we do all these things, we work hard; yes, we like it a lot, but what's the point if all the nurses and attendants aren't here?" (say the doctors). But actually, they are here; some always are, some even come in just for us even when they're not on shift, like some doctors or psychologists also do. On the other hand, nurses and doctors fire shots back and forth at each other about how their category isn't present and doesn't care: "what's the point if the nurses aren't here? . . . what's the point if the doctors aren't here?". In all of this, in the background, is the fact that the doctors at the head of the staff told me: "yes, today we'll come, also to try and push for other meetings in the future, so you can keep going next year".

After the coffee break, at the start of the second part of our meeting, I say: "let me just say, I asked myself a question; in here, exactly, who wants me to be here? On one hand there are you all, now people present that obviously want me here". That said, the discourse of the others comes out, of the absents that don't want me here and don't want to be here. The absent categories are naturally the external bureaucracies, outside the Ward, and the patients, on the inside (even though the door is open and anybody who wants to can come in).

At that moment, a patient comes in, in shorts and undershirt, a man in his 50s, athletic, fit, who in a slightly hypomanic and ironic fashion tells us:

> I'm John Wayne; since I want to get out of here; over there they told me: go and talk to doctor X [head of the department], so I'm here. They told me also: don't worry, because he doesn't do any work anyway; he's always surrounded by a lot of women and doesn't do any work.

So John Wayne enters within our group, as a spokesman of the institution; he brings several plastic bags full of food, saying: "they make us eat too much, they exhaust us, they give tons of food; I put on three kilos and I'm not doing anything; they keep me in this state I'd like to get out of, to go back home".

I think about how much John Wayne is similar to the currently absent nurses and doctors.

"I'm better and I want to get out of here" he says in an endearing manner, between the ironical and vaguely threatening. All in all, with his jeering he's saying "You (and us) are just hanging here doing nothing anyway".

Addressing the group, in which he's also now included, I say:

> There, the words of the absents have entered, the words of the institution saying: you're not doing anything here anyway; I pay you, I give you all of this free stuff and you fatten up and do nothing, what you want to do is useless so why even do it? Let's just drop it, it's better to not even go to this new burden of supervision: maybe if we go we might suffer our rage and fear from which we defend ourselves with indifference (nobody cares about me at all and me neither): the risk could be that if we become responsible we might have to work harder!

So, the persecutory depression of the whole institution is unveiled, generating indifference and inertia. Then, in a sense, the fantasy that is present at the institutional macro-levels (bureaucracy, politics) can be the one just declared here by John Wayne because of his personal history".

These things are present and can be perceived in the here and now of the group, in the institution, in the territory, but only by those with a group training in reading multilevels. Naturally when these things aren't perceived, that doesn't mean that the discourse isn't there, only that there aren't ears available that can understand that language. The institution, on its end, subconsciously thinks and even finds the languages to express itself using any of its components as a projective identification, vehicle of its languages: like the use of John Wayne demonstrates. The institution *intuitively* used him to declare, to who perceived that intuition, what was its disappointed and violent discourse toward its operators.

This is the other very important aspect of the large group: How does a large group talk? What and who does it use to talk? How then shall we listen to its language, made of words and *enactments*?

What are the users, languages and acts put on display?

A patient has entered as a patient-absent to bring the discourse of the institution-absent keeping within the discourse of the nurses-absents and the doctors-absents; it was indeed the discourse of the absents that was being realized in that moment, with the point of view of the absent also containing the "why I'm absent", brought therefore to a rational level too. It's *Intuition* that allows us to relocate all the points of view and languages back to where they've been originated: in here there's a patient who's talking; yes, he's also speaking for himself, he's telling his things, his personal matters and this can be *interpreted*. However, he's come in there speaking for others too, mainly by letting the institution's unconscious speak through his own (and this can only be intuited). This is what interests us psychoanalytically. This is the dimension of the large institutional group as a large group, that is beyond the field we're looking at and that is part of the supervision micro-group setting, but also of every other multilevel setting containing it. We can understand it only through the bi-ocularity derived by looking at "small" and "large" simultaneously. We have indeed to build a multilayer setting. If the setting was only that of the supervision room we would understand the happenings only as contents; but if the setting extends to the metasystemic containers we might be able to also understand the relation of the happenings with the contexts containing it.

Conclusions

> **Pep Esteve**: After watching the videos I wonder if we're still dreaming.
>
> **Guelfo**: Perhaps the described psychotic fields might be mythopoietical.
>
> **Participant**: I dreamt that I broke up with my partner. Then that I had a kitten with very slender fingers, a bat-kitten whose Chinese flu-like illness mixed with the witch in Hansel and Gretel. With these slender fingers I trace a contour of lines. How can one be in such a confused situation without moving over to a shape? I order my experience and I contact it as an emotion through the lines of a configuration; otherwise this would stay an ineffable experience.
>
> **Guelfo**: The me-us kitten, if it loses the group, has to build for itself, with the slender fingers of a persecutory bat, a body, a figure, a movement to keep feeling its sense of being. Will I be able to rebuild a collective body of my own, capable of dreaming and participating, not just of understanding? It's this dream that transforms into the cosmogonic myth of our group context.

The trick is fragmenting and then gluing back again: fragmenting the singular individual and collective selves, around individual dreams, then gluing them back around the myths constituting Hölldobler and Wilson's (2008) super-organisms: for example, the tale of the dance of the bees.

> **Participant**: I feel like that we have been for a while a school of sardines.
>
> **Alessandro Americo**: If one of us could be simultaneously in all the rooms of the seminar at this moment, they might catch something that goes beyond the colleagues that intervened as strangers in our group. They are John Wayne, what comes from the outside and breaks the aspect oppressing us: that we have a few minutes left while the dimension of the continuous would need dilated time. The setting, that operates a cut in reality, puts us face to face with the wound of the discrete, of the rational. Then the entrance of somebody heterogenous puts us back in contact with the

continuous. John Wayne is a revelatory mystic. Something is happening to us and he even tells us about it, because in the moment when we're in the dimension of the continuous we're also in the inexpressible. A psychotic dimension in the sense that We can forever be here as a self-interpreting group losing contact with the other side of the world. In five minutes, a cut will put us back in contact with the outside; we have a dimension in which we are trying to emotionally understand what we're experiencing and that time, as always, even if hyper-dilated, is too little. We're hungry (like the witch in the fairy tale) for someone to come saying either that it's over or that we can stay two more hours together.

Guelfo: Perhaps the real disturbance today has been the potential emergence of a thought belonging to the group; so then it's like if there had been, on one hand an expectation, almost mythical of this possibility, and at the same time a saying "it's coming; it's not". Something like awaiting that a psychotic world, dreamt in our Workshop, could be translated in a world that can be told, like this experience can, by one of us when, once we get out of here, someone will ask: "what did you actually do in there?" and the answer perhaps will be "Dunno!!!" (*laughter and mutual applause*)

References

Bion, W.R. (1977). *Seven Servants*. New York: Jason Aronson (Includes *Elements of Psychoanalysis, Learning from Experience, Transformations, Attention and Interpretation*).

Hendricks, R. (1992). *Lao Tse: Tao te ching*. New York: Ballantine Books.

Hölldobler, B., and Wilson, E.O. (2008). *The Superorganism: The Beauty, Elegance, and Strangeness of Insect Societies*. W.W. Norton.

Leopardi, G. (1818–1819). *L'infinito*. Recanati: Canti.

Margherita, G. (2012). *L'insieme Multistrato. Gruppi, Masse, Istituzioni tra Caos e Psicoanalisi*. Roma: Armando.

Matte Blanco, I. (1975). *The Unconscious as Infinite Sets*. London: Duckworth & Company.

Shannon, C.E., and Weaver, W. (1949). *A Mathematical Theory of Communication*. University of Illinois Press.

Index

122; mother's love 117, 123–124; need
of 40, 49
loved objects 38, 109, 117
lyrics 81, 83

man of achievement 80
matter 10, 27; energy-matter 137
meaning 3, 17, 44; to give /construct 67,
69, 78–79, 83, 89, 109–110, 113–114,
136–138; in hallucinosi 43; of primitive
experiences 127; quest for 44, 46–47
memory: conscious 127; emotional 5,
16, 19; opacity 26; suppression of 2–5,
10–20, 21–32, 34, 43–53, 54, 85, 121,
128
mental: state 5–6, 30, 34, 45–46, 78,
86–87, 90, 94–96, 109, 121, 123, 130,
134; suspension 27, 47, 54, 87
metaphor 6, 21, 23, 34–35, 45, 63, 88, 99,
102, 106, 122, 128
metonymy 45
Milton 34
mind: metaphorical 47, 101–103;
primordial 6–7, 54–65, 78; post-natal 1;
rational xi; state of empty 5, 11, 44, 47;
state of unsaturated 5, 44, 47, 71, 75
minus, realm of 1
misunderstanding 21–23
model 22
movement 4, 69; affective 14; dance
129–130; entropy 138; fluctuating 21;
psychic 6, 38. 90, 96, 123, 143
music 6, 80, 83, 129; composition 111;
musician scales ii
mystery 34, 90, 124, 128
mystic 87, 95–96, 138–144
mythopoietical 143; capability 33–34,
43–44, 55, 78, 86, 90, 127, 136

narration 67, 71, 110, 126, 129
negation 4–5, 10–19, 67
negative 1, 5, 7; theology 11–12
non-existence 7, 12, 27, 69, 78
notes 10–19, 25, 34
no-thing 94
nothing 94–95
nothingness 91, 95
noumena 107

O: domain of 2, 5, 43; evolution of 15, 47;
field of 137
object: dissociation good-bad 69; partial 69;
psychoanalytic 6, 86, 96; transitional 33

observation: group 34; infant (*see* infant);
psychoanalytical 4, 10, 26, 30, 55–56,
99, 127; theory 8, 131
odium *see* hate
oedipus 60
opacity of memory and desire 26, 28
openness 31, 66–67
oscillation 45, 136–138

pain: experience of 4, 88; mental 79;
physic 11, 16, 71, 119, 122; sharing 35;
tolerance to 79, 93, 122; unnecessary
8, 131
painful feelings 2, 4, 12, 19
paradigm 21, 41, 86
passion 38, 41, 95, 109, 122; com-passion
119
patience xi, 11, 55
pattern 12, 44
personality 1–2, 57, 74, 86, 110, 118, 120,
122; psychoanalytic function of 5, 43,
54, 123
perspective 2, 7–8, 30, 51, 86, 100, 102,
109
phase 46
phenomena 1, 8, 25, 43–44, 46, 52n1, 76,
100, 107, 109, 114
philosophy 141
play 37, 61–64, 66–67, 71–72, 74, 94, 111,
114, 120–121
pleasure 5, 43, 69, 79, 82, 92, 118–119
poetry 47
point 2, 8; turning 10–11; of view 76, 112,
137
position: aesthetic 70; depressive 3, 12, 21;
oscillation of Ps <=>**D** 137; paranoid-
schizoid 12, 21, 69–70
posttraumatic 103–104, 107
preconception iii, 3; innate 38, 40–41, 69
prenatal: events 56–57, 59–60; sensations
7, 57, 62
preverbal 7–8, 47, 57, 62, 127, 131
primordial mind i, 6–7, 54–65, 76–84
principle: pleasure/pain 44–69; reality 69;
of uncertainty 34
process: deduction 35; induction 35
projective identification *see* identification
protoemotions 5–6, 43, 51, 57, 71
protomental 1, 7, 57, 62, 66, 137, 140
protosensorial 7, 66–68
psychic work 12; pain linked to inability
to tolerate frustration 18, 47, 91;
rebirth 59

For Product Safety Concerns and Information please contact our EU
representative GPSR@taylorandfrancis.com
Taylor & Francis Verlag GmbH, Kaufingerstraße 24, 80331 München, Germany

www.ingramcontent.com/pod-product-compliance
Lightning Source LLC
Chambersburg PA
CBHW070344270326
41926CB00017B/3978